T0273969

HURRICANE AGNES IN VIRGINIA

EARNIE PORTA, PhD

THE
History
PRESS

Published by The History Press
Charleston, SC
www.historypress.com

Copyright © 2024 by Earnie Porta
All rights reserved

First published 2024

Manufactured in the United States

ISBN 9781467156486

Library of Congress Control Number: 2023950474

We may have the most modern technology...[but] *when nature goes on a rampage, we are its prisoners.*

—*Dr. Robert M. White, administrator of the National Oceanic and Atmospheric Administration, at a news conference on Agnes at Byrd Field in Richmond, Virginia, June 23, 1972*[1]

To my Aunt Joan, who still calls me "little Earn."

CONTENTS

ABBREVIATIONS

For the convenience of the reader, I list below the most common abbreviations used in the text. In most cases, I spell out the subject of the abbreviation when it first appears and then use the abbreviation thereafter, except in those cases where it has been a relatively long time since the abbreviation's first appearance. Additionally, throughout the text for convenience, I often refer to the Virginia State Office of Civil Defense and in particular its emergency operations center during the height of Agnes, as simply civil defense headquarters, rather than attempt where unnecessary to parse out for the reader individual components of the central state civil defense apparatus that might be taking a particular action. Finally, although I generally use "it" to describe the storm Agnes, occasionally I find it more fluid to use the pronoun "her."

COVANDAP	Commonwealth of Virginia Natural Disaster Assistance Relief Plan
HUD	U.S. Department of Housing and Urban Development
NOAA	National Oceanic and Atmospheric Administration
NWS	National Weather Service
OEP	Office of Emergency Preparedness (in the Executive Office of the President of the United States)
SBA	U.S. Small Business Administration
USDA	U.S. Department of Agriculture
VEPCO	Virginia Electric Power Company
VSOCD	Virginia State Office of Civil Defense

PREFACE

Hurricane Agnes has long held my interest. As a young boy, I remember sitting on the balcony of our third-floor apartment in Claymont, Delaware, reading a book and staring at the woods behind our building as the rain fell the entire day, preventing me from playing outside. My mother confirmed that the rain was indeed from Agnes, the storm we had been hearing about on the news. Much later in life, I moved to a small town in northern Virginia, where I learned that Agnes had been one of the most important events in the town's history, flooding much of its downtown area and destroying a beloved old bridge that had stood for almost a century.

Any number of events can pique the interest of historians, and the above explains in part why Hurricane Agnes has piqued mine. But a major goal of historians is not simply to chronicle such events but to try to make sense of them by, among other things, putting them in context, seeking to understand how they came to occur, evaluating their impact and deciding what, if any, lessons they hold for us. It is to some extent both a subjective and an artificial process, as it is more than just a description of what things happened when. With hindsight, we can link events to broader influences or outcomes, identify potential causal relationships and contemplate alternatives. But we must do so both cognizant of our own potential biases (which come simply by virtue of picking something that interests *us*) and with an awareness that for an individual or community experiencing such events in the moment, many of these linkages and relationships are unknown at the time. The intersection of cause and effect, social or individual influences on outcomes and predictable responses is often outside their line of sight. In essence, we impose a narrative that is incapable of existing at the time the event occurs.

In trying to tackle this task, I have drawn on a variety of sources. Foremost among these are the chronological accounts and reports of the Virginia Office of Civil Defense as well as those of a variety of other state agencies. Also among them are a number of subsequent reports and analyses, some shortly after the event, some a few years later and some much later. To get a more direct and detailed sense of the experience in the widespread communities in the state affected by Agnes, I accessed something we mostly do not produce anymore—the accounts of local reporters in smaller local or regional newspapers. Though it could never match direct experience, reading both these local newspaper accounts and the chronological accounts from the state Office of Civil Defense provide some sense of the alarm and confusion that must have surrounded Agnes's arrival. While fundamentally accurate and illuminating, inevitably perhaps they are at times inconsistent or contradictory, lack context, misidentify individuals or locations and contain other confusing errors. Just as one would have experienced the event itself, they reflect only a partial grasp of the situation at any given moment and one limited to the field of view of the particular observer. Through them we thus get a glimpse, however modest, of just how the event may have felt in real time.

I do not intend for this work to capture every detail of Hurricane Agnes in Virginia. Even if it was possible to do so in the abstract, it would be beyond the scope of a work of this size to cover every experience of every community in the state. But I do hope to provide a reasonably comprehensive look, one that not only examines the storm's importance within the state and nation but also reflects how varied communities and individuals experienced it firsthand in real time, outside the sweep of any overarching narrative. You will have to judge whether or not I have been successful.

ACKNOWLEDGEMENTS

While conducting my research, I used the resources of a variety of libraries and historical societies, including the Library of Congress, the Library of Virginia, the Prince William Public Library System, the Farmville–Prince Edward Historical Society, the Fluvanna Historical Society, the Goochland County Historical Society, the Nelson County Historical Society, the Occoquan Historical Society and the Scottsville Museum. The staff with whom I interacted in these organizations were always willing and helpful. Some were especially so, and I would like to mention a number of them in particular. At the Library of Virginia, staff of the Archives Reference Services and Research Room, as well Special Collections staff, assisted me greatly, especially Dale L. Neighbors, the Visual Studies Collection Coordinator for Manuscripts & Special Collections. Additionally, Betty Schneider, Senior Reference Librarian, assisted me in locating a variety of information in the Library of Virginia's collection of databases. Reference Librarian Michael T. Queen at the Library of Congress tracked down for me the Weather Bureau's 1935 Hurricane storm warning advertisement. Zoe Vitter, a friend who works at the Occoquan Historical Society, kept in mind my project while rummaging around in and reorganizing some of the society's holdings and uncovered a significant amount of seldom-used information that I found useful. And Eva Gunia at the Chinn Park Library in Prince William County helped me access microfilm resources there.

ACKNOWLEDGEMENTS

A number of people who lived through Agnes also provided me with information or reviewed portions of the manuscript, and I am grateful for their generous donation of their time. These include Kathleen Seefeldt, William Spicer, James Phelps, Maryann Phelps, Matthew Dawson, Woody Jennings, Mike Mooney and Carol Bailey.

I also want to thank all of the staff at The History Press, both for their interest in my proposal for this book and their efforts along the way. My editor, Kate Jenkins, deserves special mention and thanks for her assistance, patience and flexibility in helping me bring this work to fruition. So, too, does my copy editor, Abigail Fleming.

I would be remiss if I did not also thank in absentia all those local reporters from around the state who provided accounts of Agnes, both of the storm itself and its aftermath. We have lost a great deal with the demise of so many local newspapers. Of course, I also wish to thank those who experienced Agnes and were willing to tell their stories at the time and in later years, including those who suffered its impact and those who responded to assist those in need.

Last, but certainly not least, I want to thank my wife, Barb, who supported this project from inception to completion without reservation. This included, among numerous graces, excusing me from dishwashing duty for an extended period of time and reserving comment (mostly) when for an equally extended period of time I greatly exceeded my daily allotment of ice cream bars.

Agnes was a complex, confusing and dangerous event, and this is reflected in some of the inconsistencies in various accounts. I have tried my best to resolve those inconsistencies but no doubt failed at times. Any such failures are mine alone.

INTRODUCTION

On June 16, 1972, Vietnam dominated the headlines of Fort Walton Beach, Florida's *Playground Daily News.* One story reported the deaths of sixteen Americans in a midair explosion over South Vietnam. Another noted a temporary halt to bombing strikes near Hanoi, the capital of North Vietnam. Incongruously, below the fold on the far left of the page, UPI covered the exploits of teenager Susan Eliff of Tennessee. Eliff had broken the world rocking chair endurance record by rocking on the front porch of a country store for 125 hours and 40 minutes, "listlessly munching toast and jelly and sniffing ammonia to keep awake." After achieving her goal, a car donated by the local funeral parlor shuttled her off for an exam at a clinic before she headed to bed. Another small column from UPI, just to the right of the report on Eliff and virtually identical in length, noted that a tropical depression showed signs of strengthening into a tropical storm. Centered near Cozumel Island along the northeast tip of Mexico's Yucatán Peninsula, the storm's winds were gusting to more than forty miles per hour. The name reserved for the first tropical storm of the season, the story noted, was Agnes.[2]

Given the storm history in the state, Florida newspapers understandably paid particular attention to such weather matters. To the west of Fort Walton Beach on the state's panhandle, the *Pensacola News* briefly noted in the upper left corner of the front page that tropical storm Agnes "blew up today in the northwest Caribbean." About sixty miles to the east of Fort Walton Beach, the *Panama City News-Herald* made no mention of Agnes, but its Weekender section reminded everyone of the eleven safety tips recommended by the Red Cross now that hurricane season had started. In south Florida, the *Miami News* reported on the approaching storm at the bottom of the front page, while the *Miami Herald* placed it on page 2. Newspapers in Naples, Fort Lauderdale, Boca Raton and Tampa all printed reports on the strengthening tropical system off the Yucatán.[3]

Large newspapers on the Eastern Seaboard also took modest note of Agnes over the next couple of days. The *Boston Evening Globe* reported it on page 9 the same day as the *Playground Daily News*; a day later it landed on page 33 of the *New York Times* and a day after that appeared in Section C of the *Washington Post*. In the Southside area of Virginia, near the North Carolina border, a much smaller newspaper, the *Danville Bee*, on June 16 proclaimed, "U.S. Planes Hammer N. Vietnam," while farther down the page in the Bulletins section, an inch of type made passing reference to

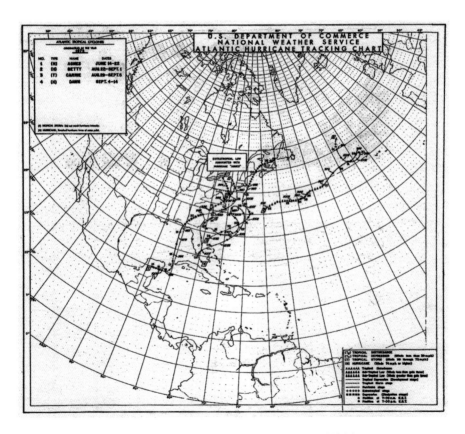

Track of Atlantic Tropical Storms and Hurricanes, 1972. *Courtesy NOAA.*

Agnes. Among newspapers large and small, however, one front page for June 16, 1972, stands out in retrospect. On that day, Florida's *Orlando Evening Star* blared in capital letters across its full width: "TROPICAL STORM GROWS."[4] Within a week, newspapers throughout the country would give similar prominence to Agnes.

For the Atlantic, 1972 was a relatively mild meteorological year. Not since 1930 had it produced so few tropical storms and hurricanes. Only four storms warranted naming, and the three that reached hurricane strength accounted for only eight total hurricane days, the second-lowest number in 30 years. Yet, the relative paucity of storms notwithstanding, 1972 was also a record year for hurricane *damage* thanks to Agnes. As Agnes traveled over land for some seven hundred miles, it "was responsible for the most damaging floods ever recorded" up to that time. More than 120 lives were lost. Estimated property damage in the United States alone totaled $3.1 billion, or more than $22.7 billion in 2023 dollars.[5]

Despite its devastating effects, Agnes never achieved the sustained wind speeds we so often associate with major hurricanes. In fact, referring to the storm as "Hurricane" Agnes is a convenient but not particularly accurate convention employed here, for it existed as a hurricane for only a short time and then only as what we would later refer to as a weak Category 1 storm.[6] Other unusual factors, however, made Agnes particularly destructive. One of these was the storm's incredibly large circulation envelope, which at times extended some one thousand nautical miles in diameter. This contained an enormous amount of moisture that fell often on already-saturated ground. Two other weather systems also contributed to making Agnes so devastating. One, an atmospheric depression to the east, accompanied Agnes on most of her journey and provided additional moisture. Another, in the form of a cold low from the Ohio Valley, later steered Agnes northward and westward, again changing the dynamic of the storm. In a sense, one might thus consider Agnes multiple storms, for it reinvented itself as it traversed the East Coast of the United States.

At first, as with most hurricanes, Agnes developed and strengthened at sea and then began to dissipate into a tropical depression when it moved inland. As a tropical depression and tropical storm, Agnes brought major flooding to western Cuba, forcing the evacuation of tens of thousands of people, damaging crops and killing seven. Briefly a hurricane, Agnes weakened as it hit Florida's Gulf Coast, where it spawned deadly tornadoes. A modest tropical depression as it crossed into Georgia, Agnes's rains brought relief to the state's farmers, who were little more than a week away from a catastrophic drought-induced crop failure. But then another Agnes emerged, one that as it moved northward grew in complexity and became rejuvenated with a capacity to drop prodigious amounts of rainfall. While crossing the Carolinas, the atmospheric activity to Agnes's east supplemented the storm, and a secondary low center emerged within the western part of the system, moving northward in tandem with the

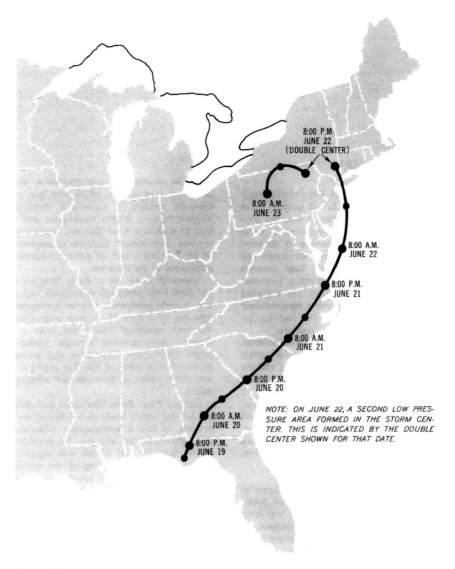

8:00 P.M.
JUNE 22
(DOUBLE CENTER)

8:00 A.M.
JUNE 23

8:00 A.M.
JUNE 22

8:00 P.M.
JUNE 21

8:00 A.M.
JUNE 21

8:00 P.M.
JUNE 20

8:00 A.M.
JUNE 20

8:00 P.M.
JUNE 19

NOTE: ON JUNE 22, A SECOND LOW PRES-
SURE AREA FORMED IN THE STORM CEN-
TER. THIS IS INDICATED BY THE DOUBLE
CENTER SHOWN FOR THAT DATE.

Path of Hurricane Agnes. *Courtesy NOAA.*

16

original low center that now shifted offshore near Norfolk, Virginia, with the result that Agnes regained almost the entirety of her previous strength. After the now powerful original low center made landfall again at Long Island, a cold low from the Ohio Valley drew Agnes inland, where her secondary low center became dominant and the storm looped back across south-central Pennsylvania before then passing through Ontario, reaching Cape Breton Island and entering the North Atlantic.[7] Eventually, after passing between Iceland and Ireland, Agnes crossed the Hebrides and disappeared, absorbed by another system southeast of Iceland.

It was after strengthening in the ocean off Norfolk, Virginia, that Agnes became most destructive. Winds were not the major culprit. Thanks in part to the contributions of the systems on either side, Agnes generated tremendous rainfall and corresponding flooding. Ten to fourteen inches fell over areas of Virginia, Maryland and Pennsylvania. Agnes hit the last of these hardest. Western Schuylkill County experienced nineteen inches of rain, and areas in Pennsylvania's Wyoming Valley and elsewhere along the Susquehanna, Schuylkill and Alleghany River basins suffered extensive damage. Pennsylvania's governor Milton Shapp evacuated his official residence by rowboat.[8] So great was the flooding that the devastation from Agnes exceeded the combined total of the two most destructive storms in history up to that point—Hurricane Betsy in 1965 and Hurricane Camille in 1969. This led two prominent meteorologists at the National Hurricane Center to describe Agnes as "the greatest natural disaster of all times."[9]

Renewed interest in Agnes has emerged in the last few years with the arrival of the storm's fiftieth anniversary. Much of the attention has understandably focused on the storm's impact in Pennsylvania. There Agnes destroyed more than two hundred bridges and over four thousand homes. Another sixty-three thousand homes suffered damage. At one point, in Wilkes-Barre, Pennsylvania, the storm trapped hundreds of people in their residences.[10] Of the more than 120 lives Agnes claimed, 48 were in Pennsylvania.

While the devastation in Pennsylvania was the most severe, this work focuses on the arguably understudied experience of Hurricane Agnes in the Commonwealth of Virginia. As noted, it was off the coast of Virginia that Agnes strengthened and nearly regained her full strength. If we conceptualize Agnes as multiple storms, or as a storm with more than one life cycle, then it was in Virginia that she began her second and most destructive phase. Fundamentally, though, the story of Agnes in Virginia is worth telling because of the effect the storm had on communities large and small; the struggles of those affected; the efforts of responders; and the lessons learned, relearned and unlearned.

Though the focus of this work is on Hurricane Agnes in Virginia, context is important. Consequently, the book begins with a look at the history and science of hurricanes to provide a fuller understanding of how they operate; the challenges they have presented; and how scientific,

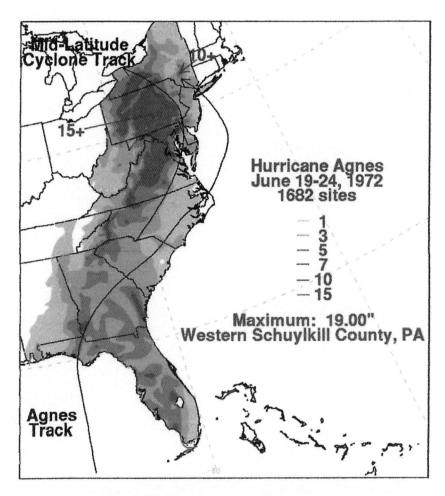

Rainfall totals from Agnes. NOAA Weather Prediction Center.

Agnes rainfall totals. *Courtesy U.S. Army Corps of Engineers.*

technological and policy advances have increased our understanding, our responses and, sometimes prematurely, our confidence. Next it addresses the conditions in Virginia before Agnes's arrival, noting the state's prior relevant experience with hurricanes, the situation in a number of communities prior to the storm and the progress of the storm northward. Then, we concentrate on the critical days in June when Agnes dumped its torrential rains. These are the days of tragedy, destruction, heroism and perseverance. The penultimate chapter looks at the difficult process of recovery and assessment before the book concludes with a review of the aftermath, not only in the commonwealth, but also in how Agnes shaped the country's approach to natural disasters. It is my hope that this account will contribute not only to a greater understanding of Agnes but also to an appreciation of the effect on the people and communities who experienced it and the place of such events in our national memory.

1

THE HISTORY AND SCIENCE OF HURRICANES

Although familiar with damaging and dangerous storms at sea, Europeans were unaware of hurricanes until they began crossing the Atlantic at the end of the fifteenth century. There they experienced the cyclonic tempests that the local Arawakan-language speakers of the Caribbean called *hurakán* after their god of storms.[11] Christopher Columbus was among the first Europeans to experience these dramatic weather events. While he had encountered powerful storms during his earlier voyages of exploration in the Western Hemisphere, it was not until his fourth voyage that it appears certain he witnessed the destructive gales the local Taino people had described to him earlier. In late June 1502, Columbus and his fleet lay in a secluded harbor on the coast of Hispaniola (present-day Haiti and the Dominican Republic), having been denied refuge in the port of Santo Domingo by the Spanish governor. Columbus had warned the governor of an approaching storm and in addition to seeking refuge had urged him to delay the departure of a large fleet bound for Spain. His entreaties rejected, Columbus sailed for safety, while the governor dispatched the Spain-bound fleet of some thirty ships. When the storm arrived, Columbus's ships were torn from their anchorages and separated, but they all survived without the loss of a single life. The homebound fleet was not so lucky. Two dozen ships sank, and more than five hundred men were lost. Only one of the ships in the fleet made it to Spain, this one ironically containing Columbus's share of cargo.[12] For the next almost 250 years, massive storms like that of

1502 continued to challenge European explorers and colonists with few advances in our understanding of them.

The first important steps toward increased knowledge of hurricanes' inner workings took place during what some refer to as the Age of Enlightenment. Two specific advances occurred in 1743 as a result of the same event, a lunar eclipse. When Benjamin Franklin stepped outside to view this particular eclipse, he found himself thwarted by clouds associated with what became known as the Eclipse Hurricane of 1743. Combining his own experience of the storm with accounts from other areas, Franklin determined that hurricanes have forward momentum and that their winds could blow in a direction opposite to the movement of the hurricane as a whole. Franklin did not understand why or how this could occur, since he was not aware of the cyclonic nature of such storms. Nevertheless, it was an important observation. A similarly important, but little understood, observation occurred when a Harvard professor of mathematics and

A Terrible and Unprecedented Storm, by Theodor de Bry, 1594. Sometimes erroneously referred to as a hurricane sinking the *Santa Maria* in 1492. *Public domain, courtesy University of Houston.*

philosophy, John Winthrop, took barometric readings of the same storm, recording the dropping atmospheric pressure that accompanied it.[13]

Almost one hundred years later, in the 1830s, two more men advanced the understanding of hurricanes dramatically. Though lacking formal scientific training, William C. Redfield became intrigued in 1821 by his observation of a hurricane's aftermath. The debris and personal accounts seemed to indicate that within a relatively small area of less than one hundred miles, the winds from the same storm had blown in opposite directions simultaneously. By further study and data accumulation, Redfield determined that hurricanes are in fact whirlwinds that blow around a central axis. He eventually formulated a relationship between the internal velocity and the forward velocity of these large circular atmospheric systems. Wind speeds in a hurricane, he asserted, increase as one moves from the edge toward the center, while at the same time the whole hurricane moves forward at a variable rate, but always slower than it rotates. Redfield explained that this meant the strongest winds will be just to the right of the center of the storm because here you will be combining both the high internal windspeeds and the forward movement of the hurricane, while the weakest winds will be to the left, where the forward movement of the storm subtracts from the internal wind speed.[14]

Working during the same period as Redfield, James P. Espy unlocked the critical role of heat in the formation of hurricanes. In tropical areas, as ocean temperatures rise, the evaporating seawater provides moisture and heat to the air above. This warm, moist air rises from the surface and continues to rise until it reaches a height in the atmosphere where it cools. Here it condenses into the clouds that eventually release the heat energy in the form of rain. While rising from the ocean's surface, the warm air also creates a low-pressure vacuum below it into which surrounding surface air rushes, in turn absorbs moisture from the ocean, is heated and rises. This continuing cycle of inrushing air that rises after being moistened and heated by the ocean is what powers hurricanes. It also explains why hurricanes weaken when they encounter land or cooler waters. There the lack of moisture and the cooler temperatures at the surface disrupt the cycle of heating that causes the air to rise, robbing the hurricane of both the heat energy it would later dispense as rain and the pressure vacuum that helps fuel its winds.[15] Although Espy made a major contribution to our understanding of hurricanes, his reputation suffered as a result of his antagonism toward Redfield, whose theories on circular wind patterns he disputed.

THE SAILOR'S HORN-BOOK

FOR THE

LAW OF STORMS:

BEING

A PRACTICAL EXPOSITION OF THE THEORY OF THE LAW OF STORMS,

AND

ITS USES TO MARINERS OF ALL CLASSES

IN ALL PARTS OF THE WORLD,

SHEWN BY

Transparent Storm Cards and Useful Lessons.

BY HENRY PIDDINGTON,

PRESIDENT OF MARINE COURTS OF ENQUIRY, CALCUTTA.

"Wherein, if any man, considering the parts thereof which I have enumerated, do judge that our labour is to collect into an art or science that which hath been pretermitted by others as matters of common sense and experience, he judgeth well."

BACON,
De Aug. Scient.

Perhaps this storm is sent with healing breath
From neighbouring shores to scourge disease and death !
'Tis ours on thine unerring Laws to trust,
With thee, great Lord ! ' whatever is, is just.'
FALCONER—*Shipwreck,*
Canto II. 884.

NEW YORK:

JOHN WILEY, 161 BROADWAY,

AND 13 PATERNOSTER ROW, LONDON.

1848.

The Sailor's Horn-Book for the Law of Storms, by Henry Piddington.

Another advance came at the hands of Henry Piddington, a former English merchant ship captain who retired to Calcutta in India, where he pursued a variety of scientific pursuits until ultimately focusing on storms. It was Piddington who coined the term *cyclone* for hurricanes in the South Pacific and Indian Ocean.[16] In 1848, he published *The Sailor's Horn-Book for the Law of Storms: Being a Practical Exposition of the Theory of the Law of Storms, and Its Uses to Mariners of All Classes in All Parts of the World, Shewn by Transparent Storm Cards and Useful Lessons.*[17] Here at last was a guide that drew on the work of Redfield and his meteorological progeny to not only explain hurricanes but also offer nautical guidance on how to avoid them, how to survive them and how to take advantage of their winds.

A couple of decades later, a schoolteacher named William Ferrel resolved the wind direction debate that had generated the antagonism between Espy and Redfield. Espy had died believing that winds rushed toward the center of a hurricane in straight lines, which conflicted with the circular whirlwind pattern postulated by Redfield and largely accepted by others. With a background in mathematics, Ferrel demonstrated that neither Redfield nor Espy was completely correct when it came to wind direction. Ferrel explained that for any body in motion, the earth's rotation would deflect it to the right in the Northern Hemisphere and to the left in the Southern Hemisphere. This meant that when surrounding air rushed in to fill the vacuum created by the low pressure at the center of the storm, the rotation of the earth deflected it from a straight path, generating the spiral associated with hurricanes.[18] With Ferrel's application to storms of what was known as the Coriolis force, after the French scientist who gave it its first mathematical expression, humanity had developed a relatively comprehensive understanding of how hurricanes worked.

Fundamental in the formation of hurricanes is an atmospheric process known as cyclogenesis, which is characterized by growing circulation around a low-pressure area. Tropical cyclones are one of the major categories of such processes, and among tropical cyclones, hurricanes are the most powerful.[19] As Paul Espy discovered, a warm ocean temperature is among the necessary elements for a hurricane's formation. In particular, the upper layer of the ocean, which descends some fifty meters, needs to achieve temperatures of approximately eighty degrees or more. This provides the moisture and heat necessary to power a hurricane. It is for this reason, along with the direction of prevailing winds, that hurricanes rarely hit the West Coast of the United States. As anyone who has gone swimming off California knows, the waters can be quite cold; they thus fail to provide the warm, moist air that powers the engine of a hurricane. A sufficient Coriolis force, as described by Ferrel, is also necessary for a hurricane to form. By virtue of the mechanics of the earth's shape and rotation, this typically requires being more than three hundred miles from the equator. Also important is some form of atmospheric instability, generally aided by high humidity at the lowest levels of the atmosphere that encourages convection (the rising of hotter, less dense air and the sinking of cooler, more dense air). Additionally, without some sort of disturbance near the surface, like a weather front, or some type of low-pressure circulation, a hurricane is unlikely to form. Finally, low vertical windshear (the difference in speed between the wind at different heights) is necessary so that the warm core can remain above the surface center of the circulation. A wind speed at higher altitudes that is much faster than at the bottom will rip the circulatory pattern apart. If all the aforementioned conditions are met, a hurricane is possible.

In the north Atlantic, most of the air masses that end up meeting these conditions originate every three to four days off the Saharan coast when the hot desert air mixes with moist air from the Indian Ocean or from the Gulf of Guinea to create areas of low pressure. After generating intense thunderstorms, prevailing winds blow these systems westward. Most dissipate. Some, however, continue west passing the Cape Verde Islands. Hence, if they ultimately develop into hurricanes, they are known as Cape Verde hurricanes. These types of storms account for about 60 percent of all hurricanes in the North Atlantic and about 85 percent of all major hurricanes. While Cape Verde hurricanes travel east to west across the Atlantic, other hurricanes originate in the Caribbean or Gulf of Mexico and travel south to north. Hurricanes can range from ten to over one thousand miles in diameter with a tranquil eye at the center when over land that may stretch some twenty to forty miles. Sometimes reaching heights in excess of fifty thousand feet, a hurricane's power is immense. It is estimated that an average hurricane generates energy equivalent to one-half of the world's total electrical generating capacity. The hurricane season in the Atlantic extends from June 1 to November 30, and among the more than twenty states hurricanes have hit, Florida has experienced by far the most.[20]

Despite Henry Piddington's advice to mariners in the mid-nineteenth century, the ability to predict and prepare for hurricanes on land lagged scientific understanding of the phenomena itself. In 1870, President Ulysses S. Grant signed into law a joint Congressional Resolution establishing what was to eventually become the National Weather Service.[21] Specifically, it required the secretary of war to provide for the taking of "meteorological observations at the military stations in the interior of the continent, and at other points in the States and Territories of the United States, and for giving notice on the northern lakes and on the sea-coast, by magnetic telegraph and marine signals, of the approach and force of storms."[22] This renewed focus notwithstanding, over the next more than fifty years, the predictive ability of personnel and instruments, as well as the ability to communicate information effectively to the communities likely to be affected, left much to be desired.

During one week in August 1893, two powerful storms struck, exposing the tracking and prediction deficiencies of what was at the time known as the Weather Bureau. One storm surprised New York City, while the other pounded the South Carolina coast, devastating the Sea Islands. A hurricane later in the year wiped out communities in Louisiana. In 1900, despite Weather Bureau pronouncements to the contrary, an even more powerful hurricane crashed into Galveston, Texas, with tragic effect, causing perhaps as many as ten thousand deaths, making it the *deadliest* natural disaster in American history.[23] Over ensuing decades, hurricanes continued to wreak havoc, particularly on coastal communities, while advances in forecasting capabilities made inadequate progress.

A number of factors led to substantive change in the 1930s. One of these was the storm season of 1933, which witnessed twenty-one storms and correspondingly poor forecasting. More importantly, as part of President Franklin D. Roosevelt's New Deal initiatives, his administration created the Science Advisory Board. Among its many activities, the board turned a critical eye toward the Weather Bureau. The Board recommended that the Bureau adopt a new airmass analysis that used upper-air data for predictions, consolidate meteorological data reporting methods, use daily weather maps more frequently and take steps toward developing long-range forecasting capabilities.[24]

It was a couple of years before the changes associated with the Science Advisory Board's recommendations took place. Among the most significant was a change in who made warning determinations. No longer would these be the exclusive province of the Weather Bureau's headquarters in Washington, D.C., with whom communicating by telegraph could result in hours of delay between the gathering, transmission and analysis of information and the eventual dissemination of warnings. This type of delay had undoubtedly played a role in the forecasting and civil defense shortcomings for storms far from the nation's capital. To address this and take advantage of local knowledge, the Bureau established new stations in San Juan, New Orleans and Jacksonville. San Juan would cover the Caribbean Sea and islands east and south of Cuba. The New Orleans station would be responsible for the Gulf Coast west of Apalachicola, Florida, while the Jacksonville station, which was later moved to Miami, would cover the rest of the Atlantic, Caribbean and the Gulf. Headquarters retained responsibility for the area starting roughly above South Carolina until 1940, when a new station in Boston assumed that function. Now hurricane warnings and forecasts would be issued four times a day and hourly when a hurricane approached land. Unlike in the past, forecasters in some stations would be on duty twenty-four hours a day.[25]

An advertising blitz in July 1935 accompanied the initial organizational changes at the renewed Weather Bureau. Full-page advertising supplements in newspapers across the country boasted, "Through New Arrangements by the Weather Bureau, Ships and Coastal Cities Will Be Able to Thwart the Fury of Storms." Substantial text, stretching across six columns of type interspersed with dramatic depictions of storms, provided detailed information on where and how hurricanes form, as well as the nature of their winds, presumably to convey that the Weather Bureau now had both intricate knowledge of these weather beasts and the capacity to defend against them. In large white letters inside the top of a massive black storm funnel, the advertisement roared, "Storm Warnings—Hurricane Coming!" Written under the byline of John L. Frazier, presumably to look more like a news article than an advertisement, the introductory paragraphs expressed the confidence the Bureau hoped to instill. "Hurricanes that roar in from the Caribbean and smite…with demon fury carrying death and destruction…are going to find it 'tough going' from now on." "Uncle Sam," the text continued in the next paragraph, "has perfected his hurricane service…perfected it to the extent of putting a decided crimp in their stealthy approach."[26] It was a bold and confident statement—and it was decidedly premature.

A little over a month later, what became known as the Labor Day Hurricane of 1935 struck the Florida Keys. It killed hundreds of World War I veterans who were living in humble shacks, sometimes only a few feet above sea level, while they worked on a government project to build a road between Miami and the bankrupt municipality of Key West. There were plenty of factors to blame for the fate of the veterans, and the inadequate performance of the Weather Bureau was among them.[27] Then, in 1938, the Weather Bureau misdiagnosed first the path and then the strength of a hurricane that slammed into Long Island and New England, killing almost seven hundred people. The resulting criticism was fierce.[28] Despite the service's shortcomings, the

National Weather Bureau advertisement, 1935. *Courtesy Library of Congress.*

reality was that reliable information on storms was still difficult to come by with the technology of the time, particularly when a storm was offshore. To do so required getting up-to-date information from maritime vessels in or close to the storm that were also in communication with the shore. For more reliable forecasting, more technological advances were necessary.

Both World War II and the Cold War subsequently spurred such advances. During the former, inadequate, easily destroyed weather balloons gave way to specially equipped aircraft that could fly into hurricanes and take important measurements. And with the advent of the Cold War and the corresponding space race, satellite technology took its place in the arsenal of tools available to observe storms and discern their path and strength.

There were also at this time substantive changes in disaster relief policies. Until the twentieth century, the public did not generally expect assistance from the federal government in the event of a natural disaster. Charitable organizations took the lead in relief efforts, and any government legislation for such aid was ad hoc. But Presidents Theodore Roosevelt and Calvin Coolidge both responded to natural disasters during their administrations with federal assistance, increasing public expectations of the national government when such events occurred. These expectations became stronger with Franklin Roosevelt's New Deal initiatives. Then, in 1950, President Harry Truman signed into law the Disaster Relief Act of 1950, which gave the president broad powers to declare major disasters and provide funds to state and local governments for infrastructure repair. Although such aid was only supposed to supplement what state and local governments could provide themselves, the act was a watershed event in the history of disaster policy, as it created what has become to this day a permanent role for the federal government in disaster relief.[29]

Not surprisingly, the extent to which presidents subsequently used this authority varied in part on their philosophy of government and in some cases on potential electoral effects. Further expanding disaster relief, Congress in 1968 passed legislation establishing the National Flood Insurance Program. The goal of the program was to reduce the long-term costs to the government of disaster relief by enabling people to purchase flood insurance that would provide compensation for loss via insurance payouts, thus reducing the need for post-disaster federal assistance. Premiums from those in flood-prone areas would fund the program. General critics of the expanding role of the federal government in disaster relief expressed worry that it would unrealistically heighten expectations for federal relief, while those opposed specifically to the flood insurance program worried that if sufficient conditions were not placed on payouts, then the program might encourage irresponsible land-use policies that would actually increase the frequency and costs of future disasters. Over the ensuing decades, critics' fears were often realized.[30]

Despite advances like "Hurricane Hunter" aircraft and satellite tracking after World War II, hurricanes continued to defy precise prediction and overwhelm efforts to guard against their destructive power. This became tragically evident again in 1969 with the arrival of Hurricane Camille, which remains the worst storm to ever strike Virginia. At first a relatively small system, Camille intensified rapidly as it headed across the Gulf of Mexico in August 1969. With barometric measurements that were the lowest up to that time taken by aircraft in the Atlantic, Camille became what we would now characterize as a Category 5 hurricane, one of only four in recorded history to strike the mainland United States. It spurned predictions that it would curve toward the Florida panhandle and instead came ashore about forty miles east of New Orleans. Camille killed more than 140 people in that coastal region and caused widespread destruction in parts of Mississippi and Louisiana. Predictably, it weakened dramatically as it moved inland through Tennessee and Kentucky. When no flooding occurred in the latter, and predictions called for no more than a maximum of two inches of rainfall in the Virginia mountains, Camille was "thought to have blown herself out."[31]

Then an unexpected development occurred. In a tragic preview of Agnes, the storm encountered other systems that altered it dramatically. A cold front forced Camille east over the Blue Ridge Mountains of central Virginia, while a westerly flow of air brought moisture from the Atlantic that was carried up the slopes of the mountains into the storm. The result was massive rainfall during the night of August 19–20 in areas surrounding tributaries of the James River on the eastern side of Virginia's Blue Ridge Mountains. Rainfall gauges in some locations were swamped and overflowed, while in others they recorded levels of twelve, fourteen or twenty-eight inches over a period of eight hours.[32]

Camille caught everyone by surprise. Rather than blowing herself out, Camille proved to be destructive and deadly. Excessive rainfall in the late hours of the night uprooted large trees and sent them crashing down mountainsides like "battering rams." Mudslides and floodwaters buried houses and swept away residents. The U.S. Department of the Interior described disaster-level flash flooding in Rockbridge, Amherst, Nelson, Albemarle and Fluvanna Counties. In Nelson County, the small village of

Massies Mill on the Tye River awoke to find few buildings left standing. As *Richmond Times-Dispatch* staff writer Lawrence Brown described it, Massies Mill once "nestled largely unnoticed in the mountains of southwest Nelson County." Now, "Massie's [*sic*] Mill didn't nestle anywhere.…Part of it was strewn across the countryside. Part of it was twisted beyond recognition. Part of it was gone." Elsewhere the rains of Camille killed multiple generations of whole families.[33]

The toll from Camille in Virginia was shocking. More than 120 people lost their lives and 37 were never found. Hundreds of buildings, bridges and miles of roadways were washed away. Flooding and mudslides caused more than $1 billion in damages as measured in 2023 dollars, with some estimates placing it as high as almost $5 billion. Subsequent analysis determined that in Nelson County alone there were nearly 3,800 landslides. A later report noted that the level of rainfall measured as twenty-eight inches over eight hours in Nelson County represented "one of the all-time meteorological anomalies in the United States," nearly matching what a Weather Bureau study from more than a decade earlier had calculated as the "probable maximum rainfall possible" in the area.[34]

As with past storms, the effects of Camille prompted review of storm forecasting and preparation capabilities. A September 1969 Commerce Department report on the warning system for the period when Camille constituted a hurricane noted approvingly that once it was identified as a developing depression in the Caribbean on August 14, personnel kept Camille under almost constant surveillance by air and satellite. When it approached land, additional resources, including weather radar, tidal gauges and human observers also contributed to surveillance. This provided some fifteen hours of advance notice to the coast, which the report's authors estimated saved fifty thousand lives. The warning system, the report asserted, "performed in an outstanding manner," and the accuracy of predictions and warnings "compar[ed] favorably with the present state of meteorological science and our present understanding of hurricanes." Authors also credited the strong cooperation of different levels of government, the news media and the public with saving lives. To the extent the experience exposed defects, the report focused on the need to develop community plans, replace equipment and capabilities destroyed by the storm and make technological improvements in specific locations along the coast and gulf basin.[35]

A separate report addressed the Virginia floods. Here the story was very different. The report described in detail the responsibilities for river and flood forecasting among various Weather Bureau offices in the region, as well as the information on which they depended. It described Camille as "a meteorological freak" when over the Virginia mountains but did not place sole blame for the resulting loss of life on the anomalous nature of the storm. Instead, the report also noted the general lack of measurement and communication infrastructure in the rural regions affected and its failure in locations where it did exist. Flooding and landslides wiped out telephone lines, so river level and rainfall measurements never reached Weather Bureau offices. Additionally, with the exception of Covington, Virginia, there were no formal community flash-flood programs in the area. Richmond's Weather Bureau office cited a variety of factors for the dearth of such systems. These included limited staffing at the Richmond office; the significant staff time needed to visit communities, convince them of the value of flood programs and then plan and supervise those programs; and the lack of funding for the necessary travel. Furthermore, given the low historical incidence of disastrous flash flooding in the region, it was a challenge to convince localities to expend resources on preparing for such events. Last, the additional instrumentation needed for an effective program was not funded.[36]

In describing the flooding, the report noted that it occurred within minutes of the torrential rainfall and that some communities actually experienced two floods—one from their immediate watercourse and another later as upstream floodwaters arrived. With little information getting to Weather Bureau offices, local police, public officials, neighbors and relatives were the main source of flood warnings, although downed telephone lines and washed-out roads obviously hampered their efforts as well. The one bright spot in the report noted that warnings reached the lower James River sufficiently in advance for Richmond to implement response plans, which included closing flood-control dikes and evacuating various areas that eventually experienced flooding.[37]

The report offered extensive recommendations for the future. Chief among these was the need to modernize the collection and transmission of river and rainfall measurements. On too many occasions during Camille, data collection and transmission hinged on a volunteer being able to get to and manually read a still-functional gauge while fighting the elements—and then find a working telephone to transmit the data. Another key finding noted the inadequacy of regular surface weather-observing stations in parts of West Virginia and Virginia; the report recommended reliable automatic weather stations to fill the gaps. To further buttress the flash-flood warning system, authors recommended that a system "based on the weather radar network be implemented in 20 states along the Atlantic and Gulf coasts and inland about 300 miles." Finally, recognizing how satellite images might have aided interpretation of the storm, the report requested that arrangements be made with NASA to use its geostationary satellite ATS-3 pictures in real time.[38]

Camille effectively exposed that hurricanes were not a danger solely confronted by coastal areas. Even with weakened winds, the moisture-carrying capacity of storms previously classified as hurricanes could wreak havoc on communities far inland, particularly where the experience with such storms was limited and the prediction apparatus and response infrastructure were weak. Memories of Camille were still fresh in the minds of many when some of the same communities affected by the storm were to experience Agnes less than three years later.

2

CONDITIONS BEFORE AGNES

Areas of Virginia had experienced major floods long before Camille arrived in 1969. After more than ten days of rain in 1771, a wall of water came down the James River and swept into Richmond. A century later in 1870, rainfall that began near Charlottesville generated massive flooding along the James, Shenandoah and Potomac Rivers. Then, to name but one more event, in 1940, a southeast hurricane caused widespread flooding in south and central Virginia. What eventually became Hurricane Agnes took shape as a tropical depression on June 14 over Mexico's Yucatán Peninsula. Of the communities in Virginia that ultimately would be affected, few took notice at that time, though for some in the south and west of the state, Camille was still a vivid memory. Like Camille, Agnes would not seriously threaten Virginia's coastal communities, instead inundating inland river basins as it unleashed its energy in the form of heavy rainfall. Unlike Camille, Agnes's reach would be extensive, with the major basins of the Potomac, Rappahannock, James and Roanoke Rivers among those experiencing the greatest impact. Each of these four river basins had played an important role in Virginia history up to that point. They would play an important role again when Agnes arrived.

Generally speaking, geographers divide Virginia into three large physiographic regions from west to east: Mountains and Valleys, the Piedmont and the Atlantic Coastal Plain or Tidewater. The westernmost, as the name implies, is mountainous and contains the subregions of the Appalachian Plateaus, the Ridge and Valley area and the Blue Ridge. In the far southwest of the state, the Appalachian Plateaus subregion includes the

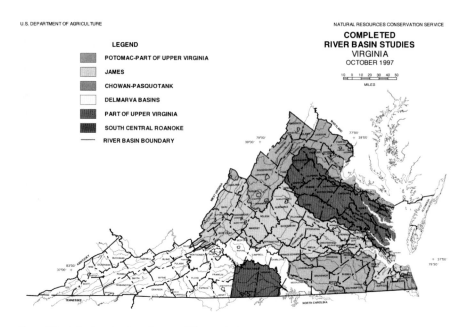

Some Virginia river basins. *Courtesy Library of Congress.*

counties of Wise, Dickenson and Buchanan and consists of an area of close mountain ranges with deep intervening valleys (for a map showing Virginia's counties see Appendix III).[39] Although none of the four major river basins mentioned above begin in this subregion of Virginia, the northernmost, the Potomac River, starts its journey eastward from the West Virginia equivalent. Immediately to the east of the Appalachian Plateaus sits the Ridge and Valley subregion, which includes the famous Shenandoah Valley. Next to it is the Blue Ridge subregion. Both the Ridge and Valley and the Blue Ridge areas have their origin in continental collisions, with the valley exhibiting more noticeably the effects of erosion and the Blue Ridge possessing a rocky core that dates back more than one billion years.[40] Together these three subregions of the Mountains and Valleys part of the state make up about 40 percent of Virginia's land area. South to north bordered on the east by Carroll, Floyd, Roanoke, Botetourt, Rockbridge, Augusta, Rockingham, Page, Warren and Clarke Counties, the Mountains and Valleys region is the point of origin for the Rappahannock, James and Roanoke Rivers.[41]

During heavy rains, communities in the mountainous areas face the twin challenges of rapid runoff from the steep topography and the collection of water in the valley floors where riverside hamlets, villages and towns are often sited. Agnes hit such communities along the tributaries of the James River, among them Covington, Clifton Forge, Lexington, Buena Vista, Massies Mill, Howardsville, Amherst and others. Some of these Camille had struck with devastating results just a few years prior. One of Virginia's largest cities, Roanoke, sits in a valley of the Blue Ridge Mountains where, bisected by the Roanoke River, it too would experience the impact of Agnes. Additionally, many creeks, streams and rivers in the Ridge and Valley subregion feed the North Branch Shenandoah and South Branch Shenandoah Rivers, which, unusually relative to most rivers, flow south to north. At Front Royal, they merge to become the Shenandoah River, which in turn joins the Potomac River at Harpers Ferry, West Virginia. Along the path of the Shenandoah and Potomac watersheds, communities like Waynesboro in Augusta County, Front Royal in Warren County, Winchester in Frederick County, the city of Alexandria in northern Virginia and the towns of Occoquan and Manassas in Prince William County would all also experience the wrath of Agnes.

When they finish their journey at the Chesapeake Bay or the Atlantic Ocean, the four major river basins mentioned do so in the easternmost physiographic region of the mid-Atlantic, the Atlantic Coastal Plain or

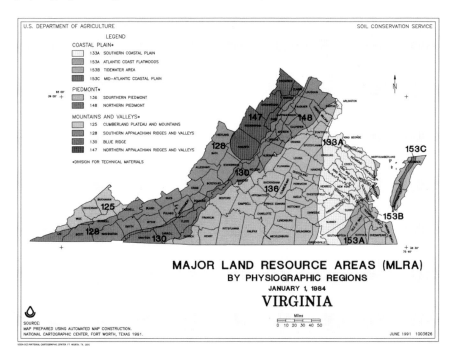

Physiographic regions of Virginia. *Courtesy Library of Congress.*

Tidewater. This is a flat, terraced area repeatedly covered and exposed over millennia by rising and falling sea levels. Making up about 21 percent of Virginia's land area, the plain generally extends no more than 250 feet above sea level at its western boundary and then slopes gradually to the coast in the east.[42] Vulnerable to flooding from oceanfront storms, Tidewater communities are often less vulnerable to raging riverine floods from the interior since the flat coastal plain, if unconstrained, allows the inland-originating waters to spread slowly out over a wide area. This was to be the case with Agnes in Virginia, where the state's coastal communities did not face the fury of oceanfront winds and rains like those in the Florida panhandle and whose flat topography reduced the speed of river-borne floodwaters from the interior.

Between the mountainous regions in the western part of the state and the coastal plain in the east is the Piedmont. Derived from a French word that means "foot of the mountains," the Piedmont makes up about 39 percent of Virginia's land area and stretches from the Blue Ridge at levels of about two thousand feet to the "Fall Line" boundary with the Coastal Plain, where river waters "fall" off the hard rock of the Piedmont to the plain below, often in a series of waterfalls or rapids.[43] Due to these rapids or waterfalls, the fall line of rivers is typically the farthest navigable point inland for large, deep-draft vessels and thus both a common place for towns and cities to form and a location where floodwaters coming from the interior sometimes flow violently with dramatic effect. The city of Alexandria and the town of Occoquan are communities sited at the fall line of the Potomac and one of its tributaries, respectively. Fredericksburg is at the fall line of the Rappahannock River; Richmond is at the fall line of the James. Petersburg sits at the fall line of a James tributary, the Appomattox River; and in the south of the state, Danville sits at the fall line of a tributary of the Roanoke River (whose fall line is in North Carolina), the Dan River. There would be many similarities in the experiences of these fall line communities during Agnes.

West of the fall line boundary between the Piedmont and Tidewater, communities also often emerged at or near a commercially useful confluence of a tributary with one of the major rivers. Culpepper and Orange, for example, emerged near tributaries of the Rappahannock before the river reaches the fall line at Fredericksburg. Additionally, as early as the eighteenth century, Virginian businessmen sought the advantages that waterways could provide for the transit of commodities from the interior. With the rivers navigable only intermittently west of the fall line, these businessmen pursued the construction of canals adjacent to rivers, by which rapids and shoals could be bypassed and waterfalls circumvented by locks. Canal projects increased the size of some communities near these confluence points and in some instances spurred the creation of new ones.

One of the largest canal projects in Virginia was the James River and Kanawha Canal, started in 1785 at the urging of George Washington. Intended to link the James River with the Kanawha River (now in West Virginia) and through it the Ohio, the Mississippi, and the Gulf of Mexico, by 1851 the canal reached Buchanan in the Blue Ridge's Botetourt County. The American Civil War and subsequent competition from expanding railroads ultimately doomed the canal project, but many communities like Scottsville, Columbia, Cartersville, Maidens and Farmville were at one time or another connected to canal projects astride Virginia rivers. All of these communities owed their existence and importance to their location adjacent to these major waterways, and Agnes would accordingly test them all.

In northern Virginia, just south of the nation's capital, the city of Alexandria sits at the fall line of the northernmost of Virginia's large river basins, the Potomac. Alexandria was once part of the land ceded to the U.S. government to form the District of Columbia, but the federal government eventually returned it to Virginia. It had been an independent city for just over a century by the time Agnes arrived. While proximity to the tidal Potomac always suggested the possibility of flood danger, the consistent threat to Alexandria had long come from elsewhere in the form of a small nine-mile-long stream known as Four Mile Run. Constituting part of the city's northern border with Arlington County, Four Mile Run was often little more than a rivulet. Yet intensive development starting in the 1940s converted almost 90 percent of the stream's drainage basin into houses, apartments, shopping centers and other urbanized areas with little open space to absorb rainfall. As a consequence, since the 1950s, floods from the stream resulted in property damage, evacuations and sometimes even death.[44]

The community of Arlandria, located in a narrow strip along Alexandria's border with Arlington County, was particularly at risk, thanks to tidal forces and a series of adjacent bridges and railroad culverts seemingly inadequate to the flow of the flood-prone stream as it traveled its final two miles toward the Potomac River. A serious flood occurred in August 1963, killing one person, forcing the evacuation of hundreds and causing almost $2 million in damages. There was another in 1966, another in 1967 and then multiple floods in 1969. In the meantime, the community of Arlandria had changed. Over time, an increasing number of residents in the once all-white enclave sold their property to Black newcomers who were seemingly unaware of the flood hazard. An Army Corps of Engineers study in 1964 deemed a flood-control program for the area not feasible, but additional floods and political pressure forced a change in viewpoint. A preliminary Corps of Engineers report in 1969 outlined a flood-control project that involved replacing the inadequate railroad culverts, enlarging the US Route 1 bridge, improving the stream channel and building levees, among other remedies. During the next year, bills to provide federal funding advanced. Hope appeared to be in the offing for those adjacent to Four Mile Run.[45]

Another ten miles or so to the south, residents of the small town of Occoquan, Virginia (population around three hundred),[46] had a great deal of affection for the adjacent river whose name the town shared. Running approximately twenty-six miles in length, the Occoquan River begins roughly in the middle of Prince William County at the confluence of two smaller tributaries, Broad Run and Cedar Run; flows in a northeasterly direction; and then about twelve miles into its journey intersects with Bull Run and turns toward the southeast. After passing the town, the Occoquan River continues east for a few miles, where it flows under bridges for Interstate 95, US Route 1 and a railway before emptying into the Potomac.

The town of Occoquan owed its founding to its location on the river's farthest navigable point, and the river had accordingly supported the town's commercial enterprises for almost two hundred years. Evidence of the community's affection for the waterway at the time was apparent in the activity of longtime town resident Rosemary Selecman. Selecman had lived in Occoquan since 1909 and sometime after World War II noticed that new signage referred to the body of water flowing past the town not as the "Occoquan River," as she and her neighbors all grew up knowing it, but as "Occoquan Creek." By April 1968, she had had enough of this apparent affront to the town and its namesake and began a persistent writing campaign, marshalling historical information to show that the waterway had consistently been identified as a river until a Fairfax County map from 1910 "suddenly" called it a creek. Over a period of several years, her extensive writing campaign won the support of local municipal governments, civic associations, historical societies, business groups and elected officials, including Virginia's powerful U.S. senator Harry F. Byrd. After a little more than three years of effort, Selecman learned in May 1971 that the U.S. Board of Geographic Names had approved for federal use the name "Occoquan River." Congratulations poured in.[47]

As with their river, residents of the town also had a great deal of affection for the bridge that crossed it at the town's northwestern end. Built in 1878, the once state-of-the-art single-lane iron Pratt truss bridge had for almost a century brought traffic and commerce through the town's main street. Refurbished in 1935, by 1972 the bridge was bringing almost 3,800 cars a day through the town on State Route 123. In the spring of 1972, however, the historic bridge was in jeopardy. Virginia's director of engineering advised that the old structure was incapable of withstanding the weights and volumes of the era's traffic and could collapse of its own weight at any time. Accordingly, the Department of Highways sought to build a new bridge on the eastern end of town that would avoid the one-lane bottleneck, as well as the ninety-degree turns, side streets and commercial entrances of the historic town.[48]

Opposition from the residents of Occoquan was intense and consistent. As a result, by early June 1972 the Department of Highways was having second thoughts. State officials noted that the estimated cost of the new bridge was growing and the lack of public support for the project raised questions about the wisdom of spending such a large sum. "Occoquan Bridge May Be Saved," reported a local newspaper. For now, it appeared, the old one-lane bridge was safe.[49]

The 1878 bridge at the town of Occoquan. *Courtesy Occoquan Historical Society.*

Near the beloved bridge, the Fairfax County Water Authority operated two water filtration plants, one on the south side of the Occoquan River in Prince William County near the town's western boundary and a second on the north side of the river in Fairfax County. Each drew water from a large reservoir just about a mile to the west of the town created by a dam built in the 1950s. A high service line also stretched across the river that could deliver water from the Fairfax filtration plant on the north side of the river to the Prince William County water distribution system on the south side.[50] Together, the two plants provided water to approximately half a million people in Prince William and Fairfax Counties, as well as to the city of Alexandria.

The Occoquan River's main tributary, the more than thirty-mile-long Bull Run, has its own storied history. Less than twenty miles northwest of the town of Occoquan, two major battles of the American Civil War occurred partly along its banks. After the war, the nearby railroad crossing of Manassas Junction just to the southeast grew into the town of Manassas and by the end of the nineteenth century had become the seat of Prince

Aerial view of Occoquan dam, treatment plants, service lines and bridge. *Courtesy Occoquan Historical Society.*

William County. By 1970, it contained approximately ten thousand people and, with the adjacent town of Manassas Park, was spurring development in county lands adjacent to Bull Run and its tributaries.

The Occoquan is but a minor tributary of the Potomac in the east. Far to the west, the Shenandoah serves as the Potomac's principal tributary, with a basin that draws exclusively from west of the Blue Ridge Mountains. There in the Shenandoah Valley the North Fork Shenandoah and the South Fork Shenandoah Rivers flow northeast on either side of the valley's Massanutten Range, until they meet at Front Royal and then continue northeast to the Shenandoah's confluence with the Potomac at Harpers Ferry. Farther south in the valley, rivers like the North, Middle and South feed the South Fork Shenandoah, and it was along the South River that Waynesboro took shape in the late eighteenth century near a gap in the Blue Ridge Mountains that made the area a convenient location for those heading to what was then the frontier of the young United States. Allegedly named in honor of General Anthony Wayne, the town of Waynesboro was recognized by the legislature in 1801 and formally incorporated in 1834. In 1865, the town witnessed Union general Philip Sheridan defeat Confederate general Jubal Early in the waning days of the American Civil War. During the early twentieth century, the town prospered and after annexing adjacent areas of Augusta County became an independent city in 1948. Dupont de Nemours became one of the city's major employers, and it was at the associated laboratory in the area that DuPont invented spandex in 1958. Over time, other communities grew alongside Waynesboro along the South River and its tributaries, including Lyndhurst, Sherando and Stuarts Draft.

Camille hit Waynesboro hard in 1969, as it did most of surrounding Augusta County. In addition to the dead and missing, five to six feet of water from the South River flooded the downtown, wreaking havoc among the businesses located there. Some found themselves trapped on rooftops and had to be rescued by boat. In the Club Court area, surrounded on three sides by a large loop of the South River, flooding inundated the community, stranding four hundred families.[51] A dozen dams interrupted the tributaries of the South River, and all of them allegedly performed well during the flooding. Critics, however, charged that the city had been delinquent in maintaining the river's channel through the town. Rather than increasing the capacity of the channel, as had apparently been requested, the town had allowed it to be filled with material, reducing its carrying capacity.[52]

Back in the eastern part of Virginia, just twenty-five to thirty miles south of the town of Occoquan, the Rappahannock River basin spreads over almost three thousand square miles, with the river itself traveling some two hundred miles as it makes its way to the Chesapeake Bay from the Blue Ridge Mountains in the west. Along its path, it encounters tributaries like the Rapidan before reaching the fall line and boundary with the Tidewater at the city of Fredericksburg. This waterway has also borne witness to the tragedy of the American Civil War, with engagements at not only Fredericksburg but also Spotsylvania Court House, Chancellorsville and the Wilderness occurring nearby.

But in the spring of 1972, those among the roughly fifteen thousand people of Fredericksburg who paid attention to the Rappahannock River were focused on a long-discussed study by the U.S. Army Corps of Engineers. For more than thirty years, the corps had been examining the idea of a dam on the Rappahannock a few miles above Fredericksburg. Known as the Salem Church Dam, the project's purported purpose would be to control floodwaters "that had ravaged the city 11 times in its 245-year history."[53] Back in 1946, however, the corps had resisted constructing a dam solely for flood-control purposes, not deeming it worth the effort absent also being built high enough to generate hydroelectric power. The project thus languished for decades until the corps eventually completed a new study in 1967. This study emphasized multiple advantages, including the creation of a reservoir encompassing some sixteen thousand acres up the Rappahannock and Rapidan Rivers. Suitable not only for recreation, the reservoir would also provide an estimated 200 million gallons of water a day to help meet the expected future water needs of rapidly growing northern Virginia. Although the dam still would not generate hydroelectric power, it could be used to flush away pollutants, help regulate salinity for the benefit of the oyster population and control flooding. As an adjunct, the corps planned to purchase twenty-six thousand acres to hold water in the event of a flood danger. At an estimated price tag of $109 million, the corps planned to seek funding and complete the project by 1982.[54]

Reactions to the project were mixed. While the corps had been urged on in the past, some local jurisdictions now bristled at the notion that they should provide water for people in northern Virginia, particularly when only Prince William County in the north confirmed it expected to need it. A number of conservation groups, led by the Conservation Council of Virginia, also opposed the Salem Church Dam, arguing before Congress that the anticipated benefits of the dam were inadequate and that the Rappahannock River should be preserved in its natural state for future generations.[55]

Another 50 miles to the south, the James River basin dwarfs the watershed of the Rappahannock. Covering some 10,000 square miles, it also stretches from the Blue Ridge Mountains to the Chesapeake Bay. With a length of 340 miles, it is the state's longest river and draws from approximately 15,000 miles of tributaries.[56] It was what one reporter characterizes as the "normally insignificant" tributaries of the James in the west, with names like Tye, Piney and Rockfish, that had devastated the communities of Nelson County in 1969 when Camille struck.[57] But Camille also affected communities along the main river's length.

One of these was Scottsville, in 1970 a small town of about three hundred straddling the Albemarle-Fluvanna County line and, like many of the towns along the James, once a port town adjacent to what had been the James River and Kanawha Canal. During the last quarter of the nineteenth century, the Richmond and Alleghany Railroad purchased the canal's right-of-way and laid tracks over the old canal towpaths. By the 1970s, these tracks were part of the Chesapeake and Ohio (C&O) railroad system.

Situated on the north bank of the James, right next to the old canal route, Scottsville had long been prone to flooding. In 1969, on the night of August 19, Hurricane Camille hammered the town with ten inches of rain. During the course of the day, floodwaters reached the second floor of some buildings, forcing the evacuation of residents, some by helicopter or boat. One observer described the town as "75 per cent under water," with the Scottsville bridge over the James partially submerged. Extensive looting of stores ensued, but generously, when the time for cleanup arrived, Mennonites from as far away as Pennsylvania assisted, refusing payment. In fact, the Mennonite Disaster Service, a volunteer organization from Mennonite churches in the eastern United States, assisted in several locations. Some forty to fifty Mennonite volunteers in the Stuart's Draft chapter of the organization helped with the cleanup in the Club Court area of Waynesboro. Led by the state director of the organization, the Stuart's Draft chapter also sent volunteers to Nelson County, Buena Vista in Rockbridge County and elsewhere.[58]

In the spring of 1972, the chief concern in Scottsville appeared to be noise. As the mayor explained at the town's May 15 council meeting, there had been "numerous complaints concerning speeding cars, blowing of car horns and unnecessary noise that disturb the peace" on Sunday when the town sergeant was no longer on duty. When the meeting concluded, people gathered to seek a solution. But the destruction wrought by Camille a few years earlier had not been entirely forgotten in the area. The report on the council meeting also noted that Vernard Hurt, whose home in the small village of Howardsville about eight miles to the southwest had been washed out by Camille and then destroyed by fire, has "the framework up on a new house" thanks to the work of volunteers. He now had need of sheetrock, wiring, a refrigerator, a table, chairs, a stove and bed linens. Contributions, the *Farmville Herald* reported, could be made to the "Vernard Hurt Building Fund."[59]

About twenty miles to the east of Scottsville, the small town of Columbia stood at the confluence of the James and Rivanna Rivers astride Virginia State Route 6. A town since 1788, Columbia prospered for a time as a tobacco shipping port, much like other towns along the canal route. By the mid-twentieth century, however, Columbia was in decline. When it came through in 1969, Camille wiped out one span of a nearby bridge and covered the north bank of Route 6, dealing a blow to the community. By 1972, Columbia consisted of little more than one hundred people.

Another ten miles to the southeast, on the south side of a bend in the James, the small community of Cartersville had also formed around the James and Kanawha Canal project. Though Camille forced the closure of the Route 45 bridge across the James there, Cartersville itself appeared to have largely escaped significant damage. In April 1972, the state announced it was allocating funds for the improvement of the bridge and its approaches on both the Cumberland and Goochland County sides.[60]

About fifteen miles to the east of Cartersville on the north bank of the James, yet another community had taken shape in part as a result of the James and Kanawha Canal. In 1972, Maidens existed as a small commercial community down a slope along the banks of the James River adjacent to the tracks of the C&O Railroad. There, a railroad station and other buildings suffered during Camille but remained. And although the storm damaged the bridge across the James, by the spring of 1972 a new bridge had been installed, with the old one slated for demolition. State plans announced in April of that year called for the expenditure of an additional $275,000 for construction and right-of-way acquisition for the bridge and its approaches.[61]

Thirty miles to the southeast sits the state capital, Richmond. There the Fulton Bottom neighborhood in Richmond's east end had seen better days. The community of 190 acres contained nine hundred mostly Black families, bounded by East Main Street, the James River, Government Road, Orleans Street and Powhatan Hill. One of Richmond's earliest communities, Fulton Bottom was once the home of craftsmen, workmen and shopkeepers. But a study in the 1960s by the Richmond Redevelopment and Housing Authority (RRHA) claimed that "the years that have swept over Fulton Bottom have battered it into a state of virtual ruin. Age, neglect, abuse and the encroachment of industry have transformed Fulton Bottom into a slum, the worst in Richmond." A journalist wrote that "though many may see

Fulton Bottom, and shudder momentarily at what they see, few know what it really is like. For it is a community apart, a pocket of misery in a generally healthy, prosperous and happy city....Most of the misery of Fulton Bottom is hidden in its dark and dismal houses." Many of the houses allegedly lacked indoor plumbing. According to the recommendations of the RRHA, Fulton Bottom was beyond hope of rehabilitation and should be razed and redeveloped mostly for industry, with some new residences and low-rent public housing.[62]

Fulton Bottom residents reacted negatively to the report's characterization of their community. A local church leader acknowledged that the social cohesion of the community had decreased in recent years with a growth in transients. But this, he noted, had occurred in part because of a redevelopment project elsewhere in Richmond that had pushed people out of their community with no realistic alternative other than moving to Fulton Bottom. The city was also to blame, he remarked, for its failure over many years to enforce the housing code. This was a problem acknowledged by at least one city official, who attributed enforcement deficiencies in part to the belief that the area would ultimately be redeveloped.[63]

Representatives for the residents of Fulton Bottom originally supported the Richmond City Council's decision in late 1966 to fund the RRHA study but expected greater resident involvement in the planning process. With almost half of the dwelling units owner-occupied and only half of those qualifying as dilapidated, community leaders thought a base for rebuilding existed. Eventually, residents and the RRHA hashed out a plan that called for a renewal effort that would result in a community 40 percent residential, 20 percent industrial, 15 percent parks, 10 percent commercial, 10 percent major roadways, 3 percent schools and 2 percent churches. Despite assumptions to the contrary, however, there was no firm commitment to rehabilitating, as opposed to replacing, current structures.[64]

The residents of Fulton Bottom also faced additional challenges in their struggle to maintain their sense of community identity as they tried to navigate the calls for urban renewal. Along with Shockoe Bottom, an adjacent low-lying riverside section of Richmond to the northwest, Fulton Bottom experienced periodic flooding from the James River. When Camille arrived in August 1969, Richmond received enough warning about rainfall and flooding in the western part of the state to prepare for the downstream impact. Residents evacuated as Shockoe and Fulton Bottom flooded.

Sixty miles to the southwest of Fulton Bottom, the town of Farmville sits near the headwaters of one of the major tributaries of the James River, the Appomattox. As the county seat of Prince Edward County in 1972, Farmville counted among its populace approximately one-third of the county's total population of almost fifteen thousand. When it passed through central Virginia in August 1969, Hurricane Camille missed Farmville, dropping most of its rainfall to the northwest. Appreciative of their good fortune, the town's residents and businesses responded generously to the needs of surrounding communities that had not been so lucky. A drive by the town's Jaycees generated an estimated five tons of food for Camille's victims, as well as clothing and household goods. Dozens of Farmville volunteers participated in search and rescue, cleanup and disaster relief. Trucks, heavy equipment and hand tools from Farmville assisted with the removal of debris.[65] Established in the late eighteenth century, like many of the towns along the James mentioned earlier, Farmville was also once associated with a canal system, which was used to ship commodities to Petersburg until the coming of the railroads. By the 1970s, however, Farmville was far more well known for its role in the struggle over school desegregation.

In 1951, students at Farmville's all-Black R.R. Morton High School protested the terrible conditions at their school and the refusal of the county's appointed all-white school board to remedy the situation. The court case resulting from these protests was one of those consolidated into *Brown v. Board of Education* (1954), where a unanimous Supreme Court overturned the "separate, but equal" doctrine on which segregationists had long relied. Rather than acquiesce to the court's rulings, Virginia resisted. Adopting the policy known as "Massive Resistance," the state government refused to desegregate the schools. Federal courts responded, forcing the admission of Black students to white public schools. As a consequence, in 1959 the state abandoned the formal Massive Resistance program. But Prince Edward County officials still refused to comply. Rather than admit Black students, the county school board instead closed all public schools; whites then used state tuition grants to establish private schools open only to them. Not until 1964 did the courts force the Prince Edward County public school system to reopen, and not until after 1968 did another U.S. Supreme Court case force large-scale desegregation.

In the 1970s, more than one-third of Prince Edward County residents were Black and unfortunately, in the spring of 1972, they were still fighting the battle over school desegregation. On March 17, 1972, the *Farmville Herald* printed a scathing editorial opposing the then almost twenty-year-old decision in *Brown*. It criticized the Supreme Court for having "left the Constitution and substituting their own socially-oriented opinions" and criticized Congress for falling "into the trap of penalizing one segment of the nation—the South." To the editorial board, the time had come, "as this unholy web spins around the North, the East, and the West," for a constitutional amendment.[66] When the Prince Edward County Democrats announced that they had met the new full participation rules of the latest Virginia Democratic Party Plan, which required that delegations to the party's state convention in June contain women, members of minority groups and young people in reasonable proportion to their presence in the population, the *Farmville Herald* responded with a bitter editorial titled, "Democratic Suicide."[67]

While the struggle over civil rights continued to be debated in Farmville in the spring of 1972, the town and surrounding area were in the midst of a building boom. An annexation of some two thousand acres from surrounding counties went into effect in 1971, significantly increasing Farmville's size. Residents then approved in overwhelming fashion a $3 million bond issue for the construction of a new water treatment plant and extension of water and sewer lines. Officials signed a contract in April for extension of the lines to serve the south end of town, and work was expected to begin shortly thereafter. In the meantime, fueled largely by new homes, building in Farmville and Prince Edward County proceeded at a record-breaking pace, nearing almost $2 million by early June. Major state transportation projects planned for the area, the *Farmville Herald* reported, included the Farmville bypass and the rebuilding of Routes 15 and 460 at the town's west end.[68]

The state was also providing another type of aid. In March 1972, the Piedmont Planning District Commission appointed a former staff writer of the *Farmville Herald*, James E. Harris Jr., to lead an effort to develop a prototype civil defense plan that would improve counties' ability to work together during natural disasters or "enemy attack." Funded by the State Office of Civil Defense, the project also involved the University of Virginia. At a subsequent meeting in Farmville, officials outlined how the seven counties and two towns in the district hoped to provide an example for the rest of the state and country; whereas the old system was geared toward an enemy nuclear attack that never came, this one would focus on natural disasters, "which come regularly" and for which communities are unprepared. At the same time as this was happening, the Farmville Composite Squadron of the Civil Air Patrol reactivated.[69]

As Agnes approached, in its June 21 issue, the *Farmville Herald* carried a small news item on the second page noting that five days prior, "Five men, four identified as Cuban nationals and one as a former employee of the CIA and FBI, broke into the Washington headquarters of the Democratic

National Committee."[70] There was no mention of the impending storm. That would change very soon.

Another eighty miles to the west of Farmville, in a large valley of the Blue Ridge Mountains, the Roanoke River flows through the city of Roanoke. The river's drainage basin rivals that of the James, covering approximately ten thousand square miles. Originating in the mountains, it travels over four hundred miles, with almost half of that occurring in North Carolina where it enters Albemarle Sound. Although the river winds its way in several large bends through the city, residents generally did not appear to worry over much about flooding. Camille's destruction missed Roanoke in 1969, and the city's civic organizations contributed to relief for those affected elsewhere. To the extent flooding was a topic of conversation among the city's 90,000-plus inhabitants in the spring of 1972, it appeared focused on the February 26 disaster in Logan County, West Virginia, where after heavy rains three of the Buffalo Mining Company's coal-waste dams on Buffalo Creek collapsed, killing more than 120 people in a deluge of dark water. Residents could read regularly in the *Roanoke Times* about the disaster, as well as the ensuing wildcat strike by more than 1,000 West Virginia coal miners in June.[71] Roanoke, like all the communities mentioned, whether or not they had experienced Camille in 1969, would feel the force of Agnes.

Prior to the arrival of Camille, civil defense plans for much of the 1960s bore the hallmarks of a focus on the threat of nuclear war. In fact, when speaking to a Roanoke Kiwanis club after Agnes, Erskine White, deputy regional director of the Virginia Office of Civil Defense for Western Virginia, remarked that when Camille arrived almost the only civil defense plan Virginia had "was the plan for use after a nuclear attack."[72] This was consistent with the Federal Civil Defense Act of 1950, which declared it the policy and intent of Congress to provide a plan of civil defense for the protection of life and property in the United States in the event of enemy attack. Furthermore, under the act the primary responsibility for civil defense was to rest with the states and their political subdivisions, with the federal government providing "necessary coordination and guidance" and assistance where authorized. Nowhere in the act did civil defense activities mention responding to natural disasters.[73] In contrast, Virginia's civil defense legislation in 1952 specifically covered "time of war, grave national peril, or *serious natural disaster*" (emphasis in original).[74] Despite this broader mandate in Virginia, the focus on the threat of enemy attack continued to dominate civil defense considerations in the state through most of the 1960s. As a result, as the threat of such attack appeared to fade, the local civil defense apparatus stagnated. With the state government supporting half the cost of local civil defense programs, some jurisdictions simply used the state funds to offset the cost of existing personnel to whom they had assigned some pro forma civil defense responsibilities.

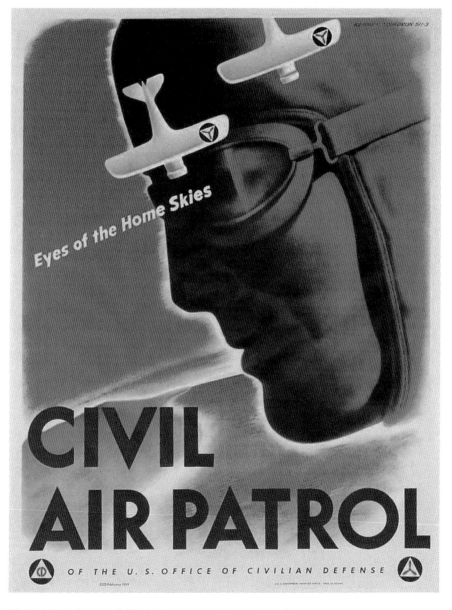

Civil Air Patrol poster. *Public domain, courtesy of Boston Public Library.*

Camille exposed in dramatic and deadly fashion the weaknesses in this approach, highlighting not only the limits of a narrow focus on nuclear war or enemy attack but also the inadequacies in personnel and training. After the administration of Governor Linwood Holton took office in 1970, the governor's civil defense coordinator, Thomas P. Credle, reportedly claimed that Camille "shook the civil defense agency to its very foundation."[75] With the shortcomings in Virginia's civil defense apparatus thus made evident by Camille, the Holton administration determined to improve the situation. On May 5, 1972, the governor signed and issued the new Commonwealth of Virginia Natural Disaster Assistance Relief Plan (COVANDAP), dated March 1972, which established policies and procedures for operations in the event of a natural disaster anywhere in the state.

Reflecting a comprehensive view of civil defense, COVANDAP defined a natural disaster to include any "hurricane, tornado, storm, flood, high water, wind-driven water, tidal wave, earthquake, drought, fire or other catastrophe resulting in damage, hardship, suffering, or possible loss of life." The plan acknowledged that the primary responsibility for responding to such events rested with state and local governments and should be addressed at the lowest level of government possible, with federal disaster assistance supplementing those efforts only in circumstances in which state and local resources were insufficient to meet the need. Accordingly, the plan's stated objective was to assist "state and local government officials with the actions required should a natural disaster occur; outline the procedures necessary to become eligible for Federal assistance; explain the provisions and statutory requirements of... the [federal] Disaster Relief Act of 1970; and...outline the aid or assistance available to individuals, business establishments, and State and local governments."[76] In the words of Coordinator Credle, the aim of the plan was to provide "an instant comprehensive response" to a local disaster and to offer state assistance in "any situation that exceeds the capability of local governments."[77] With the state divided into three Civil Defense Regions and twenty-two planning districts, if a disaster struck Virginia, the declaration of an emergency by the governor would trigger obligations on the part of specific state agencies for a wide variety of disaster-response activities in affected areas. It was a comprehensive approach designed to meet a broad range of challenges, which the state tested on December 7, 1971, in an exercise dubbed "Katy." A little more than a month after the plan's formal promulgation, and a little more than a week after its distribution around the state, Agnes would offer a true test.[78]

3

AGNES ARRIVES

JUNE 14–JUNE 20

On June 14, 1972, observations of lower atmospheric pressure around Cozumel, in the Mexican state of Quintana Roo, augured the beginning of Agnes, and a day later the National Hurricane Center began initiating advisories on the forming tropical depression. In the parlance of the National Hurricane Center, a tropical depression is a cyclonic storm in the tropics with maximum sustained winds of thirty-eight miles per hour (thirty-three knots). When those sustained winds reach a level of between thirty-nine and seventy-three miles per hour (thirty-four to sixty-three knots), the storm is formally designated a tropical storm and assigned a name. If winds reach a sustained level of seventy-four miles per hour (sixty-four knots) or more, the storm is characterized as a hurricane. As this particular tropical depression curved slowly northward toward the Yucatán Channel, which separates Cuba from the Yucatán Peninsula and the Caribbean from the Gulf of Mexico, its wind speeds increased, and the National Hurricane Center labeled the system a tropical storm and assigned the name reserved for the first storm of the season—Agnes.[79]

As is the case now, the names for major storms at that time were determined before a storm season began and were assigned in order. By late April 1972, the National Hurricane Center had released fourteen names reserved for use in the upcoming season: Agnes, Betty, Carry, Dawn, Edna, Felice, Gerda, Harriet, Ilene, Jane, Kara, Lucile, Mae and Nadine. Unlike today, the names available were exclusively female. Since 1953, the United States had been using only female names for storms, and this practiced continued until 1978 for eastern North Pacific storms and until 1979 for the Atlantic and Gulf of Mexico. Today, the World Meteorological Organization controls the naming of storms. Its lists repeat every six years and alternate use of traditional male and female names. Some storms are so deadly or costly, however, that their names are retired, not to be used again. Agnes was one such storm.[80]

As the Hurricane Center ordered reconnaissance flights into Agnes's center, reports emerged of the damage it was inflicting on Cuba. Stalling for a time between the western end of the island and the Yucatán Peninsula, Agnes forced evacuations in the western Cuban province of Pinar Del Rio. More than two thousand people (a number that would eventually grow to more than thirty-five thousand) relocated, as did thousands of food animals. Flooding reportedly consumed close to eleven thousand acres of agricultural fields, affecting rice, vegetables, sugar and tobacco crops. It was in Cuba that Agnes also claimed its first lives, when four men drowned in a reservoir on

ATS-3 satellite image of June 12, 1972, before Agnes formed. *Courtesy NOAA/NWS.*

the Isle of Pines as the rain flooded and overturned their small boat. The death toll in Cuba later rose to seven.[81]

On June 18, Agnes became a hurricane while still in the Gulf of Mexico, achieving sustained winds of approximately eighty-five miles per hour (seventy-four knots). But it weakened quickly as it approached landfall, with the director of the National Hurricane Center reportedly describing it as "big, flat nothingness." When it finally came ashore near Cape San Blas in the Florida panhandle on the afternoon of June 19, Fort Walton Beach and Panama City Beach escaped significant damage, with the mayor of the latter reportedly grumbling, "We've had worse storms in winter."[82] Others were not so fortunate.

On the coast, Agnes flooded some low-lying areas, hitting Apalachicola particularly hard. But it was mostly the tornados Agnes spawned in various places that made her deadly in Florida. In Okeechobee, for example, a tornado destroyed three trailer parks, killing at least five people and injuring dozens of others.[83] As it crossed into Georgia on June 20, however, Agnes no longer even qualified as a tropical storm; weather officials had downgraded it to a tropical depression. Here it was greeted by some with relief, as it "drifted benignly" across the state with slow, soaking rainfall providing much-need water for south Georgia's drought-stricken crops. (Just a week prior, three Georgia counties had sought emergency assistance due to drought.) With winds down to around twenty-five miles per hour as the storm crossed into South Carolina and eastern North Carolina, a public relations spokesperson for the Georgia Farm Bureau referred to Agnes as a "$100-million rain for Georgia farmers." According to the spokesman, in some parts of the state, another ten days without rain would have led to catastrophic crop failure. "This was a life saver," he claimed. Officials also credited Agnes with cleaning pollution from the air above the city of Atlanta. Thanks to the rains and winds of Agnes, the figure for June 20 was the lowest recorded since authorities began measuring pollution in the city just two years before.[84]

But as Agnes moved into the Carolinas, something unexpected occurred. As meteorologists Robert Simpson and Paul Herbert would later describe it, other weather systems helped rejuvenate Agnes, transforming it into a far different storm than what Georgia had experienced. In the western Atlantic, a ridge of high pressure continued to build, and a major extratropical (i.e., outside the tropics) trough approached Agnes from the east, spurring acceleration with central pressure once again falling. Meanwhile, early on June 21, west of the center of Agnes, a secondary low center developed, which then moved in tandem with the old center, helping Agnes again

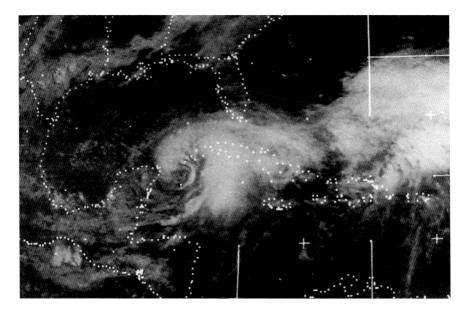

ATS-3 satellite image of June 17, 1972, as Agnes reached hurricane status. *Courtesy NOAA/NWS.*

reach tropical storm strength while still over North Carolina. This new low eventually became dominant and remained inland, but not before Agnes moved offshore of Norfolk, Virginia, and on the evening of June 21 regained almost her entire strength.[85]

In North Carolina on June 20 and 21, what were then still considered remnants of the prior tropical storm dumped rainfall in the mountains that caused landslides, flooded roads and bridges and forced evacuations to higher ground. Of the more than 120 fatalities attributed to Agnes, 2 occurred in North Carolina. While South Carolina experienced some river-borne flooding, Agnes caused no fatalities and relatively modest damage there.[86] As the storm moved off the coast at Norfolk, however, things would be different in Virginia.

It had already been raining in parts of the state for days when on the afternoon of Tuesday, June 20, Virginia's State Office of Civil Defense (VSOCD) and the Department of the State Police went on alert status, activating their warning networks and contacting civil defense, police and other officials in the state. Located at 7700 Midlothian Turnpike, just outside Richmond City limits, civil defense headquarters operated the state's emergency operations center during the ensuing natural disaster until closing the operation on June 29.

On June 20, the National Weather Service issued a flash-flood watch[87] in the early afternoon for Montgomery, Giles, Carroll and Craig Counties in the southwestern part of the state between the mountainous border with West Virginia and the North Carolina line. Later in the evening, it also issued flash-flood warnings for Albemarle, Amherst and Nelson Counties, all areas particularly hard-hit by Camille nearly three years before. At the same time, the State Police reported that the Piney River—one of the small tributaries of the James that had caused so much devastation during Camille—was five feet above normal. Within minutes, civil defense headquarters passed this information on to the local civil defense coordinators in Albemarle, Amherst and Nelson Counties and thereafter as well to the sheriff's departments of the three counties and to Virginia's civil defense coordinator, Thomas Credle.[88]

No doubt with Camille in mind, local officials in Nelson County reacted swiftly to the approach of Agnes. As early as the afternoon of Tuesday, June 20, state police and sheriff's deputies advised evacuation and found that in the area surrounding the small communities of Massies Mill and Tyro on the Tye River, people did not need to be told; they were evacuating on their own initiative. Officials established refugee centers at the Woodson School in Lowesville near the Piney River, the Temperance School in Amherst County about a mile away and one in the Roseland Rescue Squad building, not far from the Tye River. By Tuesday night, the centers reportedly housed some fifty people, and officials alerted the Red Cross chapters in Amherst and Nelson Counties.[89] Near midnight, reports arrived that Route 56 outside of Massie's Mill was blocked, as were roads above Lowesville along the Piney River. As a result, the Nelson County Sheriff's Department reported, four of its cars would be on the road throughout the night, as would two state police troopers and a state police sergeant. They were, in the estimation of Civil Defense Region II's assistant regional coordinator, William Whitehead, "on top of it."[90]

Soon after the Office of Civil Defense began operations on the early afternoon of June 20, the coordinator for Region I, Donald Glenn, reported that in Pulaski County, bounded on its north, east and south by counties under a flash-flood watch, it was cloudy with light rain, but there were no problems. On Wednesday, June 21, that would change. That was the day Agnes moved off the Virginia coast, strengthened and regained its former strength as a tropical storm, its rains reaching all the way to Upstate New York.

JUNE 21

On Wednesday, June 21, the summer solstice and longest day of the year, the State Office of Civil Defense changed from "alert" to "emergency operational" status, essentially transforming into a round-the-clock operation. Regional civil defense coordinators headed to likely problem areas with instructions to provide hourly updates on conditions and to coordinate the delivery of resources. As emergency operations staff received these updates, they posted them on a situation board, provided them to action officers and used a statewide road map to provide a visual display of where there was trouble. Increased civil defense readiness came with support from the Coast Guard, Army National Guard, state entities, the Virginia Association of Rescue Squads and the Civil Air Patrol.

Civil Defense Region I stretched from Lee County in the far southwest of the state to an eastern boundary that arced from Alleghany County on the border with West Virginia to Pittsylvania County on the border with North Carolina. In between on its eastern edge it included Botetourt, Bedford, Amherst, Appomattox and Campbell Counties, thus including much of the Roanoke River basin as well as some of the southernmost tributaries of the James. Donald Glenn, the Region I coordinator, had been monitoring heavy rainfall from his office since 4:00 a.m. At 7:00 a.m., he reported that there were no problems in the extreme southwest of his jurisdiction in places like Lee, Scott and Wise Counties, but troubling signs were emerging elsewhere.

Calls had come in from the Montgomery County civil defense director and sheriff as early as 3:00 a.m. attempting to evaluate reports from people leaving the area who claimed that others might have been cut off as flooding from a tributary of the Roanoke River affected Route 637. To investigate such reports, a call went out to the Salem division of the state police to see if a helicopter flyover was possible. This was to be among the first of many anecdotal reports that would present a recurring challenge to civil defense personnel. Observations of private citizens on the scene or evacuating an area, if accurate, could provide invaluable, lifesaving information. If not accurate, or exaggerated, however, they could lead to a misallocation of resources that might have deadly consequences. Throughout the disaster, civil defense personnel had to determine the reliability of such information and make quick decisions in real time.

Reports and requests began to come in rapidly to civil defense headquarters during the daylit morning hours of June 21, with Amherst, Nelson, Alleghany and Craig Counties all reporting some flooding. Just to the southwest of Montgomery County, things had changed overnight in Pulaski. Incorporated in 1886, the town of Pulaski, named after the Polish hero of the American Revolution, Count Casimir Pulaski, served as the seat of Pulaski County. Prior to the town's founding, Peak Creek meandered through the area. Not part of any of the east-flowing river basins of Virginia, Peak Creek flows into the New River, which in turn flows north and west to the Kanawha, the same river to which Virginia canal proponents of the eighteenth and nineteenth century hoped to connect the James. As the town took shape, in the early 1900s, workers straightened the creek and lined it with native limestone. Floods in 1929 and 1954 spurred calls to both straighten the creek further and deepen its bed to increase carrying capacity and reduce flood risk. At the recommendation of the U.S. Corps of Engineers, the town eventually implemented the changes, straightening and deepening its path.[91]

Light rain in Pulaski did not initially cause problems. But as in other locations in this part of Virginia, it had been raining in Pulaski since Saturday, and those three prior days of rain had left the ground saturated, with little capacity to absorb more. The initial light rain of June 20 continued into the nighttime hours, and by day's end an additional reportedly 2.85 inches had fallen, which by dawn the following day amounted to 3.60 inches of rain in a twenty-four-hour period.[92] This was simply too much for Peak Creek, which overflowed its banks. Evacuations of families at the lower end of the Dora Highway began at about 5:30 a.m. on June 21. By 8:00 a.m., about seventy-five people had to be evacuated from their homes in the Kersey Bottom area off Commerce Street, where water had risen in some places to heights of three feet. Not long after, the power went out when almost three feet of water drowned the Appalachian Power Company's electrical substation.[93] Losing contact with Pulaski's National Guard Armory, civil defense headquarters learned it was among the buildings that had flooded. In all, rescue squads reported evacuating more than one hundred people from their homes in the town and county on June 21. To the town's east, where Peak Creek flowed into Claytor Lake, dam workmen, conscious of the flooding risk, spilled water to lower the lake by four feet so that downstream communities of the New River into which the lake emptied remained largely unaffected.[94] Officials were proud of the efforts of responders, with the executive secretary of Pulaski County, Robert McNichols, noting that he "had never seen better cooperation of the police, sheriff's department, Red Cross and rescue units than their efforts" on June 21.[95] There would be many more opportunities for responders to perform as well elsewhere in the state.

To the north of Pulaski in the Roanoke Basin, the first substantive report from the city of Roanoke did not arrive in civil defense headquarters until much later in the day; at a little after 9:00 p.m., the National Guard Armory there advised it was surrounded by more than 2 feet of water. At the time, officials reported they expected the Roanoke River to crest around midnight at a level in excess of 22 feet.[96] In fact, however, the river had already crested at a record 19.35 feet and was receding rapidly. Among the most heavily hit parts of the city was the Jefferson Street area between the Jefferson Street Bridge and the Roanoke Memorial Hospital.[97] At the hospital, employees filled and placed 1,800 sandbags, which helped limit flooding to the parking lot and to some water seepage in the hospital basement.[98] Nearby Victory Stadium, however, lay under six feet of water. Flooding eventually caused the closure of about a dozen streets, but the city avoided deaths and serious injury.[99]

Disaster responders in Roanoke were among the first who had to deal with some of the same needless distractions that would occur in many other communities struck more aggressively by Agnes. While search and rescue operations were difficult enough in their own right, law enforcement personnel also had to deal with the twin problems of looters and sightseers. In Roanoke, the former appeared to be of only modest concern. At one point, lumber from a storage area and nearby construction site became dislodged by floodwaters and floated down Roanoke Avenue. Police found looters swimming out to the pieces, bringing them to dry land and then trying to make off with them; police put a halt the practice.[100] Concerns about looting, however, sprang up again and again in flood-stricken communities. On subsequent days, officials reported looting and, in some cases, requested National Guard support to contain it, in Manassas (where thieves allegedly used boats to gain access to flooded buildings),[101] Waynesboro, Scottsville, Columbia, Farmville and Petersburg, among others.

Sightseers were another problem. Police expressed their dismay at the conduct of some, whose curiosity hindered evacuations and rescues and, in some cases, elevated the risk to disaster response personnel. Pulaski residents of two flood-prone areas, for example, complained to police that sightseers were hindering their attempts to evacuate furniture and household goods from the impending flood's path.[102] In Charlottesville, officials warned people of the danger posed by exposed power lines in flooded areas and asked the curious to refrain from visiting flooded areas lest they hamper rescue and cleanup efforts.[103] A fire administrator and civil defense coordinator in Manassas also cited sightseers as a source of difficulty[104] When

Farmville eventually requested National Guard support, it was not only to prevent looting, but also to keep crowds out of the floodwaters, and when floodwaters eventually reached Richmond, the National Guard had to clear four to five hundred gawkers out of Chimborazo Park.[105] First responders were particularly appalled by parents who allowed their children to wade in the floodwaters of urban streets, seemingly oblivious to the dangers created when stormwater surges popped off manhole covers, creating unseen holes in the street below the opaque waters.[106] Officials in some areas issued strong warnings against swimming or wading in flooded areas, citing concerns that extended beyond the dangers posed by the deceptive strength of the current or sewage contamination, noting that snakes and other wild animals, forced from their natural habitat, could be lurking near the water's edge.[107]

Immediately adjacent to Roanoke, the city of Salem, the seat for Roanoke County, reported at 1:30 p.m. that it had opened its National Guard Armory. As with the city of Roanoke, the Roanoke River flows through Salem, but by 4:30 p.m., officials there were apparently experiencing no problems they felt it necessary to report to civil defense headquarters. Their only remark was that it was no longer raining. Yet much like Roanoke, Salem ultimately found itself confronting a dozen flooded streets, as well as a natural gas tank explosion at a trailer park and a group of sixth graders stranded at a YMCA camp to the south.[108]

Southwest of Roanoke and Salem, floodwaters from the South Fork Roanoke River hammered the small communities of Alleghany Springs, Shawsville and Elliston. Evacuations began in the rain at 2:00 a.m., and within a few hours, the water reportedly was rising five feet every half hour. With the roads washed out, helicopters rescued the residents of Alleghany Springs. Refugees from trailer courts along Route 11 found comfort at local churches, Shawsville High School and the Meadowbrook Nursing Home.[109] Northeast of Salem and Roanoke, on the James River just east of the Blue Ridge Mountains, June 21 saw 6.02 inches of rain in the city of Lynchburg, and at 8:30 p.m., Lynchburg reported a level of twenty-four feet, six inches, on the James River, six and a half feet above flood stage.[110]

North of Pulaski and Roanoke, and along and west of the Blue Ridge Mountains, reports arrived at civil defense headquarters after noon describing high water and slides blocking roads in Rockbridge, Augusta, Bath and Alleghany Counties.[111] In the last of these, the Jackson River, a tributary of the James west of the Blue Ridge Mountains, threatened the low-lying areas of the cities of Clifton Forge and Covington, ten miles from each other and another ten from the West Virginia border. Earlier, at 10:30 a.m. the Jackson

River at Covington, normally about two and a half feet deep, was twelve feet above normal and reportedly rising at the rate of more than a foot an hour. Dunlap Creek, which intersects the Jackson River on Covington's western border, was fifteen feet above normal and rising even faster. Floodwaters forced the closure of a bridge leading to several nearby subdivisions, and first-aid crews rescued residents of trailers along another tributary of the Jackson River, Potts Creek. By noon, floodwaters had swamped the electrical station, and the power went out in the city, forcing businesses to close and preventing the *Covington Virginian* newspaper from publishing.[112] As the situation deteriorated in Alleghany County, in neighboring Craig County to the south floodwaters necessitated the rescue from Camp Easter Seal of 136 people by boat, among them 66 children with disabilities, many of them in wheelchairs.[113] In the midst of all this, at 12:15 p.m., the National Weather Service reported that rain would continue for another eighteen to twenty-four hours in amounts potentially exceeding five inches in mountain areas and with major flooding likely.[114]

As with Rockbridge, Augusta, Bath and Alleghany Counties, just after noon, reports came to civil defense headquarters that in Amherst County several bridges had washed out and rockslides were blocking parts of Route 60.[115] Understandably, concerns thus also increased about neighboring Nelson County, the epicenter of devastation during Camille. Again, the normally "insignificant" tributaries of the James—the Rockfish, Tye and Piney—were becoming threatening, as would the James herself. As after-action reports noted, however, unlike during Camille, most of the flooding from Agnes in Nelson County took place there during daylight hours, so people were "not trapped in their homes during the night or faced with a wall of water" as they had been when Camille struck.[116] Floodwaters from Agnes also rose more slowly than did those of Camille. Although both factors worked to the relative benefit of Nelson County residents, perhaps most importantly the memories of Camille were fresh in their minds and they thus reacted quickly to Agnes. As the rain continued and the longest day of the year wore on, the numbers in the area's refugee centers grew. People evacuated Norwood and Wingina along the James.[117] By 1:30 p.m., people in the county seat of Lovingston had started to leave their homes. More than 70 people evacuated Massies Mill and the surrounding areas of the Tye River, and almost 150 left Lowesville and the Wheeles Cove–Davis Creek area near the Piney River.[118] The people of Nelson County clearly remembered Camille. Among those who chose a different course of action, at least temporarily, was U.S. postal carrier Shirley Cash. Out delivering her mail as usual on June 21, partway through her route, high water forced her to abandon her car, at which point she trudged through the woods to continue delivery, sometimes to residents who had already fled the area.[119]

Whereas in Nelson County Agnes was more forgiving than Camille had been, fifty miles to the southeast on the Appomattox River at the town of Farmville, which had escaped Camille's wrath, that would not be the case. At 1:27 p.m., James Harris, civil defense planner for Planning District 14 of the Piedmont Planning District—the same James E. Harris Jr. who used to work for the *Farmville Herald*—reported to civil defense headquarters that "Farmville had several businesses flooded and that two feet of water covered Route 460."[120] The Appomattox River bordered Farmville to the north, while its tributary Buffalo Creek bordered the town on the west. A small stream flowed roughly through the center of town before emptying into the Appomattox. With the rainfall Agnes was to bring and the location of these three watercourses, the situation in Farmville deteriorated throughout the day.

When passing through Farmville on June 21, Agnes reportedly dropped 7.49 inches of rain in a twenty-four-hour period. This was part of an unbroken stretch of twenty-six straight hours of rainfall, which sent the Appomattox River over its banks by more than the twenty-three feet recorded in a flood in 1940. Floodwaters eventually covered the Route 45 bridge, blocking access to the town from the north, while to the west, the Appomattox and its tributary Buffalo Creek blocked the town's main western approaches. Route 15 to the south now offered the only path for evacuation. In the meantime, rising water backed up the creek flowing through town, flooding areas of Second, Third, Fourth and other Streets and inundating stores, car dealerships, gas stations and the A&P. Farmville also experienced an impact from Agnes that was to afflict some other communities struck by the storm and that would linger and cause concern after the rains stopped and the skies were blue and bright. At about 4:00 p.m. on June 21, the rising waters from Buffalo Creek forced the shutdown of pumps at the local water plant. Workers used sandbags and stayed at the plant as long as they could on Wednesday night in a futile attempt to protect both the plant's equipment from water damage and the water well from contamination. After midnight, however, rising floodwaters forced the workers to abandon the effort. Until the waters receded and the plant equipment and clear water well could be sterilized, the town would have to rely on the water available in storage tanks located on higher ground.[121]

The bridge across the James River at Wingina. *Courtesy Library of Virginia.*

As the afternoon continued, reports reached civil defense headquarters detailing the river gauge readings along the James and its tributaries: 21.6 feet at Licks Run in Alleghany County and 19.0 feet, 2.00 feet above flood stage, at Buchanan in neighboring Botetourt County to the southeast. At Buena Vista in Rockbridge County just to the northeast, the James rose more than half a foot or more an hour as it approached the flood stage of 17.00 feet.[122]

As the storm moved north and east, so too did the focus of attention. A little before 5:00 p.m., the National Weather Service issued flash-flood warnings for Fluvanna, Louise, Goochland, Buckingham and Orange Counties while also leaving in effect those previously issued for the counties in the mountainous west. Before 6:00 p.m., the Weather Service also warned of major flooding potential for the James and Rapidan Rivers and northern Virginia. With the latter came to headquarters the first reports of storm-related deaths in the state. On Route 60 in Buckingham County, an Illinois man, his wife and reportedly two children with them died when their car was swept into the James River.[123] Not long after, Nelson County reported the death of seventy-nine-year old Robert Roy Henderson, whose car ran into a washed-out culvert of Taylor Creek on Route 633. In fact, although it would not become known until later, June 21 was Agnes's deadliest day in Virginia, accounting for ten of the storm's deaths.[124] Homer Wilson Comer was found drowned near his home in Page County. Francoise M. Craig, while firemen attempted to get her to higher ground, was swept away by the swollen waters of Accotink Creek in northern Virginia's Fairfax County. Also in Fairfax County, retired schoolteacher Frances Sandford Davis was found in a cow pasture near Pleasant Valley Road, and Michael Dennis Robeys died when his car was swept away by the floodwaters of Difficult Run. Active-duty soldier Ovis Willard Whytsell died at Fort Belvoir in Fairfax County in a flood-related automobile accident. As these first tragic reports arrived at civil defense headquarters, the Weather Service expanded its flood warnings, adding Spotsylvania and Hanover Counties, followed later by Henrico, Chesterfield and Caroline Counties as well.

On the James River, trouble arose as the river rose. In Albemarle County's tiny community of Howardsville—a handful of stores and dwellings virtually wiped out by Camille—people moved belongings to upper levels

Route 645 bridge repair near Norwood. *Courtesy Library of Virginia.*

in an attempt to avoid damage as the community was once again awash.[125] There, Vernard Hurt, the same Vernard Hurt whom the *Farmville Herald* reported had the frame going up on a new house thanks to the efforts of volunteers, was among three individuals evacuated from mobile homes that were allegedly later seen floating down the James River.[126]

In Scottsville, on top of a large northern bend of the James, Agnes dropped some ten inches of rain on June 21. Observers quickly characterized the situation as worse than that of Camille almost three years earlier, noting that a plaque placed on the post office to mark the height of Camille's floodwaters was already nearly covered. Water rose rapidly, and as darkness arrived and 10:00 p.m. approached, Scottsville reported it had reached ten feet on Main Street.[127]

Fifteen miles to the north of Scottsville, another tributary of the James, the Rivanna River, threatened the city of Charlottesville in the evening hours of June 21. Of particular concern was Long Street's Free Bridge, which carries Route 250 over the river. Floodwaters inundated areas in the southeastern part of the city, and as the rains continued, more than

Floodwaters in Farmville shown from the corner of Third Street. *Courtesy Library of Virginia.*

Rooftop floodwaters in Farmville. *Courtesy Library of Virginia.*

fifty people, among them campers, tourists and visitors, sought refuge in a recreation center staffed by the Red Cross and civil defense personnel. The city council called an emergency meeting with department heads to prepare for potential problems. Rain stopped at midnight, and although in the early morning hours of the next day the waters of the Rivanna River rose high enough to crash over the Free Bridge, additional evacuations did not become necessary.[128]

A few of the newly warned areas, and some, but not all, of those to the north and east, appeared to be managing relatively well on their own. Officials in the city of Waynesboro in the Shenandoah Valley had been preparing for Agnes since at least June 20, with memories of Camille reportedly in mind. The residents along Back Creek and the South River were the most vulnerable. Carefully monitoring rising water levels, the town sent police door-to-door beginning at 4:00 a.m. on June 21 to warn residents in flood-prone areas of the potential threat. Later in the afternoon, police closed some roads and noted flooding was making some other streets hazardous.[129] Reporting a little before 7:30 p.m. that the South River was rising at the rate of one foot per hour, local officials advised civil defense headquarters that they could handle the situation.[130]

Although officials in Waynesboro indeed proved they were largely capable of handling things themselves, the situation during the day had not been as uneventful as the report to civil defense headquarters might suggest. Before it began to recede between 7:00 and 8:00 p.m. on the evening of June 21, the South River crested at a level approximately 13.5 feet above normal, flooding the downtown area and turning it into what one observer described as a "veritable lake" dividing the city roughly in two.[131] In the interim, Waynesboro area officials also found themselves confronting two potential catastrophes. One was among the first serious reports in the state of a potential dam failure. Although recorded in the civil defense headquarters chronology as a threat from water flowing more than a foot over the flashboard of the "Sherando Lake Dam near Stuarts Draft," this appears to be inaccurate in terms of both its location and its characterization.[132] Multiple subsequent press reports indicate that the dam in question was actually the Augusta County Service Authority's Coles

View of Scottsville floodwaters. *Courtesy Library of Virginia.*

Reservoir Dam, several miles closer to Stuart's Draft and feeding a tributary of the South River that ran through the eastern side of the community. But regardless of the accuracy of the initial report, the threat was real.[133]

A five-foot-high "flash board" sat atop the earthen dam of the Coles Reservoir. It was designed to give way and relieve pressure on the dam when the water reached dangerous levels. The reservoir's contents approached that point on the afternoon of June 21.[134] Concerned about the possibility of the flashboard (and perhaps even the dam) giving way, officials sent the Waynesboro Police and First Aid Crew out into areas most at risk. Using loudspeakers, they urged people to evacuate in twenty minutes and, seeing some residents start to return to their homes, allegedly directed them not to go back for anything, exclaiming over the loudspeakers, "You may lose your life."[135] Once again, as with Camille, the residents of the Club Court area, surrounded on three sides by a loop of the South River, found themselves in harm's way; after the loudspeaker warnings, most promptly evacuated the area, leading one observer to subsequently describe Club Court as a "Ghost Town."[136] Evacuations proceeded in other areas around Waynesboro, including both in nearby Sherando, close to Back Creek, as well as in Stuart's Draft.[137] From the latter, officials evacuated some 150 people from Ridgeview Acres, Suburban Heights and other subdivisions. First feeding almost all these evacuees at a school in Stuart's Draft, officials then sent them to spend the night at local homes and at a church staffed by the Staunton National Guard.[138] Records from civil defense headquarters reflect a request from the county sheriff for a helicopter to rescue individuals in the Sherando area satisfied by the dispatch of high-clearance National Guard trucks able to navigate the floodwaters.[139]

A second potential crisis emerged in the Waynesboro area around 4:30 p.m. when a 1,200-gallon tank of propane broke loose and floated into a collection of stacked lumber. With the tank spewing gas, authorities feared it might strike other objects, resulting in an explosion. The Waynesboro Fire Department and First Aid Crew inched a boat toward the tank, eventually successfully securing it and closing the tank's open valve.[140] By 7:30 p.m., the situation in Waynesboro had stabilized; the Coles Reservoir Dam held, and the waters of the South River were receding.[141]

More than a dozen miles north of Waynesboro on Route 340, the small towns of Grottoes, Elkton and Bridgewater also experienced flooding. The South River flooded about eight blocks of the Dogwood Avenue section of Grottoes, leading to the evacuation of about a dozen families. Another dozen or so miles north along Route 340, where Elk Run flows into the South Fork

Shenandoah River, floodwaters forced closure of the intersection between Route 340 and Route 33, covering some of the downtown area of Elkton with two to three feet of water and reportedly entering a number of stores. North of Waynesboro about twenty-five miles up Route 254 and Route 11, the North River flooded the central part of Bridgewater, and a little more than another twenty-five miles north, floodwaters on Route 340 cut off the north and south approaches to the town of Luray, the seat of Page County.[142]

About the same time that Waynesboro reported conditions there had stabilized, in adjacent Albemarle County twenty miles to the east, floodwater cut off two routes into the city of Charlottesville. Another twenty miles to the northeast in Orange County, floodwaters cut off the town of Orange as well.[143] Though as we have seen there was flooding in Charlottesville, neither locality reported significant problems. Unknown to civil defense headquarters, however, quick action by a resident of the Gordonsville area of Orange County headed off a potential railroad catastrophe. Just south of the town of Gordonsville, the Superior Stone Company operated a 110-foot-deep quarry covering ten to fifteen acres. A Chesapeake & Ohio Railroad line ran adjacent to the quarry, and when the heavy rains of Agnes arrived, the track bed behaved as a de facto dam, holding back water draining from the west. Eventually, the water undermined the track, leaving the rails suspended in the air; over the next several hours, the now rushing waters from the west filled the quarry. Luckily, a former Gordonsville town official witnessed the failure of the ad hoc dam and alerted the railroad communications office in Gordonsville so that rail traffic could be diverted.[144]

Moving fifteen more miles north along Route 15 into Culpeper County, the town of Culpeper seemed to be managing. Its six thousand inhabitants were isolated, with a number of surrounding roads under water. Flooding from small streams had also forced evacuation of a trailer park and motel, but there were no deaths or injuries, and fewer than fifty people needed to use the two schools opened as shelters. Yet another twenty miles northward up Route 15, sheriff's deputies in the Fauquier County seat at Warrenton reported that water in some of the town's streets was covering automobiles and was reportedly ten feet high in places; they estimated more than one hundred homes would be total losses. Police, firefighters, sheriff's deputies and rescue personnel assisted hundreds of people in stranded cars as Cedar Run, a tributary of the Occoquan River, washed over sections of Route 15 and Route 29, rendering them impassable.[145]

At the north end of the Shenandoah Valley, in Warren, Clarke and Frederick Counties, people were wary. The Shenandoah River was not expected to crest until the evening of the next day. Warren County's Sheriff's Department personnel worked continuously, evacuating people from subdivisions and campgrounds near the river. Authorities also closed almost all the access roads to the Shenandoah in Clarke County, while in the city of Winchester in Frederick County, Abrams Creek overflowed its banks, and water overloaded the sanitary and storm sewers, flooding several streets and a few businesses. In the Blue Ridge Mountains, National Forest Service personnel searched for stranded campers. For Berryville, the seat of Clarke County, the impact was modest, though reportedly almost every basement flooded.[146]

At civil defense headquarters during the evening hours of June 21, reports continued to come in from a variety of sources, including amateur radio net operators and members of the general public. With the increasing number of reports came an increasing need to evaluate and filter them for reliability. At 7:20 p.m. in the west end of Richmond, for example, there was a report of a tornado, which turned out to be the roar from a nearby dam. Ten minutes later, a doctor reported inaccurately that the water supply in Lovingston had been contaminated. Two hours earlier in Covington, an oil tank ruptured and was reportedly leaking gas into the Jackson River. About an hour later, the National Guard sealed the leak, but it seems clear the incident raised apprehensions in Covington, for at 7:30 p.m. the Civil Air Patrol reported that a gas line had burst there and the Alleghany County hospital was being evacuated. This turned out to be another false report; civil defense regional personnel investigated and determined the gas main had been shut off due to a bad valve—the hospital was not being evacuated. Just before 9:00 p.m., an unconfirmed and ultimately erroneous report of two deaths in Covington made its way to civil defense headquarters as well. A few minutes later, the Red Cross provided a reliable update of the situation in the city. At what amounted to day's end, there in a valley of the Appalachians, the Red Cross reported that roughly a third of Covington, some eighteen square blocks, was flooded, affecting about three hundred homes, and that evacuees were being housed in shelters, hospitals and nursing homes, with food available to all.[147]

Although the situation remained tense in the steep-sloped, mountainous counties in the western part of the state, as well as in communities farther east that were awaiting downstream effects, as the storm moved north, stability spread in some of the more southerly areas. While the city of Danville, adjacent to the North Carolina border in Pittsylvania County, had not featured prominently in any reports to civil defense headquarters, it was one of the Virginia localities hit early by the rains from Agnes. The Dan River snakes back and forth across the Virginia–North Carolina border before it eventually reaches the Roanoke and on its journey passes through the center of Danville. During a twelve-hour span beginning at 1:00 a.m. on Wednesday, June 21, Agnes dropped 3.67 inches on Danville. As with other areas in the state, it had been raining off and on in Danville since Saturday and the ground was already saturated, limiting the amount of additional rainfall the ground could accommodate. Ultimately, the Dan River exceeded its record flood level, reaching more than nine feet above flood stage, but the resulting flooding from the river and its tributaries, while inconvenient, lacked the devastating effect flooding from Agnes was to have elsewhere. Roads and bridges became blocked, both by floodwaters and backed-up stormwater systems, and had to be closed. Basements flooded, as did yards, parking lots and outdoor storage areas, and there were limited power outages. Danville's Life Saving and First Aid Crew reportedly assisted four children and two adults stranded in about five feet of water. Yet for the most part, public safety personnel managed traffic disruptions, while residents, business owners and utility operators made do with sandbags and water pumps, limiting damage.[148] By 5:00 p.m. on June 21, Danville reported to civil defense headquarters that it did not expect any additional problems. A short time after, the town of Pulaski also reported that its situation was stable and no additional help was needed.[149] Meanwhile, in Nelson County there was now very little rain; small streams were receding; food was being distributed; and almost two hundred evacuees were sheltering in schools, churches and stores or staying with friends.[150]

As the true dark nighttime hours of the first day of summer finally descended, many locations seemed to have weathered the worst. Waters had crested and were receding in multiple locations. Shelters were in place and providing housing, food and clothing to those who had been displaced. Red Cross personnel were on alert and in contact with their local civil defense coordinators. Overall, for some anyway, the situation appeared to be well in hand, and the *Richmond Times-Dispatch* noted, "By tonight, the weather service forecast, cooler air from the west, coupled with the movement of the tropical depression offshore, will bring fair skies to Virginia once more."[151] As the darkness deepened, however, and the longest day of the year came to a close, there were troubling reports out of northern Virginia. In Prince William County, things were not going well. Agnes was not finished.

The first information from Prince William County came to civil defense headquarters a little after 7:00 p.m., with a report that floodwaters had broken a small dam near Bull Run Mountain, possibly resulting in one death. Unfortunately, this proved to be true, as authorities later identified the body of Lorenza Harris, twenty-nine, of Haymarket, Virginia, who died when a small earthen-filled dam in the Jackson Hollow recreational area gave way.[152] Within a half hour, the Fredericksburg Police Department, located in the county immediately to the south, reported the town of Manassas had lost power and that many parts of Prince William County were flooded.[153] At the Prince William County National Guard Armory in Manassas, the officers of Company A, Third Battalion, 116th Infantry, were meeting on the evening of June 21 to finalize plans for the upcoming annual guard camp when they received a call from the county police asking for assistance. Guard officers opened the armory as a shelter and by 11:00 p.m. reported that about thirty people were under their care, including a number of people simply passing through the area. Prince William County's armory, however, was not prepared to serve as a shelter, and soon after opening the power went out. With an electric-powered water pump, the power outage left the armory with no water for drinking or sanitary needs. As more people arrived, the guardsmen worked by flashlight and gas lantern, but it soon became apparent that they needed food and blankets for the arriving refugees.[154] A request for bedding, food and medical care arrived at state civil defense headquarters at 11:29 p.m. A minute later, the last report to civil defense headquarters for June 21 arrived. It simply but ominously stated that the "town of Occoquan was evacuated into Manassas with the Red Cross to follow-up in the morning."[155]

By day's end, all state agencies with disaster responsibilities had been advised to increase their state of readiness and had been briefed once more on the Commonwealth of Virginia Natural Disaster Assistance Response Plan (COVNDAP), while the Office of Civil Defense was on full alert and operating around the clock. The National Weather Service issued a late bulletin reporting that heavy rains had increased the flooding threat to the James River basin to a level equal to that of Hurricane Camille. It advised continued "emergency preparations and evacuations to the fullest extent possible."[156] From its earliest moments on Thursday, June 22, Agnes would put Virginia's civil defense apparatus to the test.

JUNE 22

Like many river-valley communities tucked close between a hillside and a river, the town of Occoquan was vulnerable to flooding from multiple sources during periods of extended heavy rainfall. Tributary streams were one source of flooding, a problem some residents attributed to residential and commercial development in upland areas that now fed runoff to the streams, causing them to overflow their banks and effectively turn the town's streets into new, temporary tributaries as the floodwaters flowed rapidly downhill to the river. The river itself was also a source of flooding when heavy rains to the west or a tidal bore from an ocean storm caused it to overflow its banks running parallel to the town's main street. Indeed, the rainfall from Agnes generated concern about both, as "torrents" of water flowed through the streets from nearby hills and the level of the Occoquan River continued to rise. As conditions worsened, town residents heard a knock at their door that when answered revealed a firefighter telling them it was time to leave—immediately. Occoquan was being evacuated.[157]

Ultimately, approximately five hundred people from Occoquan and the surrounding area sheltered, not in Manassas as originally recorded by civil defense headquarters, but at the Botts Fire Station in nearby Woodbridge, where Salvation Army volunteers and the Ladies Auxiliary of the Occoquan-Woodbridge-Lorton (OWL) Volunteer Fire Department registered them; set up bunks; and provided food, baby's milk and games donated by local businesses, civic associations and the U.S. Army and Marine Corps. As one assistant fire chief reportedly remarked, although not planned that way, the fire station "had become the disaster headquarters for Eastern Prince William County." As time wore on, the de facto disaster headquarters became overcrowded, and authorities began to house arriving refugees from the storm in a nearby Masonic Lodge and in area churches. In the meantime, firefighters from the station also had to respond to calls for help from elsewhere—a flooding trailer park, for example, and people stranded by swift floodwaters, trapped in their cars, standing on truck cabs or hanging from tree limbs.[158]

But as troubling as the potential for flood damage from the streams and river was, the issue of most serious concern for the town of Occoquan in the late evening hours of June 21 was neither the tributary streams nor the river but instead the threat from the Occoquan dam. Located about a mile to the west of the town, the fifty-five-foot-high dam created a large reservoir that provided drinking water for the rapidly growing communities of northern Virginia. The structure, however, was not a flood-control dam. At its north end there was a spillway, but there were no gates to quickly regulate the flow of water. Shortly after midnight, at 12:18 a.m. on June 22, the National Guard reported that the Occoquan dam might break. To make matters worse, less than fifteen minutes later, an ambiguous report arrived in civil defense headquarters from the state police. Interstate 95 remained open to the District of Columbia, according to the report, but there was "mention of a problem of a barge against a bridge somewhere along I-95," with the location of the barge unknown. Just before 1:00 a.m., the state police reported the closure of I-95 and US Route 1 in Prince William County.[159]

Chief Tommy Furr of the Occoquan-Woodbridge-Lorton Volunteer Fire Department had been involved in aiding three men who had ignored a roadblock on US Route 1, tying himself together with others and wading into the swift waters to perform the rescue. According to reports, he also happened to be in the town of Occoquan when he witnessed a barge break loose, crash into a large boat and a dock—upending the former and destroying the latter—and then continue downstream. Worried about it potentially damaging the downriver I-95 bridge, he sent a team to close off the interstate. Men from the fire department were on the bridge when the barge struck, generating "a tremendous thump" and causing the pillars of the bridge to vibrate.[160] A press account characterized the barge's effect on the bridge as "tilting it precariously," and another claimed authorities said the bridge was "damaged significantly" and "may go out."[161]

On this second full day of activity at civil defense headquarters, reports arrived fast and furious throughout the early hours, and from northern Virginia, most of the news was not good. Although headquarters does not record receiving any reports, the night before, the city of Alexandria, just south of the nation's capital and adjacent to the Potomac River, witnessed a flurry of activity. As early as 8:05 p.m., authorities ordered the evacuation of some one thousand people in the Arlandria section of Alexandria, adjacent to Four Mile Run. An hour and fifteen minutes later, Four Mile Run reached its ten-foot flood stage, rising at the rate of an inch a minute. Overflowing its banks, it tore through Arlandria. On the southwestern side of Alexandria, Holmes Run also exceeded its banks, and by 10:15 p.m. abandoned cars floated down both waterways.[162] At 11:00 p.m., a fire broke out at the Beverly Plaza Shopping Center on Mt. Vernon Avenue in

Arlandria. With floodwaters eight feet deep in front of the stores, firefighters could not reach the blaze. Within a few hours, six stores in the center had burned to the waterline.[163] Ultimately, the Civil Air Patrol reported helping 150 people evacuate Arlandria.[164]

Occoquan's dam was also not the only dam causing concern in northern Virginia. The same Holmes Run that ran through the western and southern portions of the city of Alexandria also fed and emerged from Lake Barcroft, near Bailey's Crossroad's in Fairfax County. Barcroft owed its existence to the damming of Holmes Run and another nearby stream. With water levels rising and coming over the dam on the evening of June 21, authorities ordered evacuation of about eighty homes. Within an hour of the evacuation order, water eroded the earth on the west end of the concrete dam and the lake began pouring into the valley below. In response, the Army Corps of Engineers dispatched men to sandbag and reinforce the face of the dam. By 2:00 a.m., the level of the lake had fallen by ten feet and officials concluded the danger had passed.[165]

While officials worried about two dams in northern Virginia, reports continued to arrive in the early morning hours that painted a fuller picture of the disaster occurring elsewhere in Prince William County. By 3:00 a.m., the National Guard reported that Routes 234, 28, 15 and 66 were all closed and that the guard was sending additional men and trucks to the area. According to reports, more than 1,600 people were now refugees in Prince William County, sheltered in schools, fire stations and the National Guard armory. Among these were people displaced by the Bull Run tributary of the Occoquan, whose floodwaters on Wednesday had submerged most of the 140-unit Bull Run Trailer Park near Route 28 in the northern part of the county, sweeping some of the mobile homes away in the process. Floodwaters from Bull Run and its tributaries also inundated the Westgate, Sudley and Yorkshire subdivisions south of the river above the town of Manassas Park. Firefighters waded through high water to rescue people from their homes. In one incident, three county police officers obtained a fourteen-foot motorboat and rescued three women who had fled to a public phone booth and closed the door hoping to avoid being swept away. An earlier attempt at rescue by men in a dump truck failed when the dump truck itself was swept away. As the water in the phone booth rose and the women reportedly stood on their toes to keep their heads above it, rescuers from the Stonewall Jackson Fire Department arrived in the boat and secured both the three women and the men who had been swept away in the dump truck.[166]

Response activities in western Prince William County appeared less well-coordinated than elsewhere, understandable given that civil defense training had been scheduled but not yet held.[167] When the flooding began on June 21, observers witnessed county and town police and volunteer firefighters go into action right away to save lives. But when asked who was coordinating rescue operations, one fire department leader reportedly responded, "Unfortunately no one. We're all doing the best we can."[168] At the National Guard Armory in Manassas, the commander had, as noted earlier, made the armory available as a shelter on being contacted by the county police. But the actual request from the police sought National Guard assistance in rescuing forty-three Girl Scouts from Connecticut who were in Prince William Forest Park. The guard commander reportedly responded that he would have to get approval from a higher authority to perform rescue missions but, in what was likely a humanitarian example of exceeding his authority at the time, offered to keep the armory open for people who were stranded. The Girl Scouts rescued themselves, leaving their tents behind when the waters threatened and taking refuge in the Dumfries-Triangle Fire Station social hall.[169] Approval for the guard to assist in rescue operations did not arrive until just before midnight. Even then, it was unclear who would be coordinating operations. Nevertheless, to their credit, when a call came in from Manassas Park to assist with the flood victims south of Bull Run, the guardsmen headed out; on site, order was established among the multiple responders with different agencies assuming primary responsibility for different types of activities.[170]

Of course, as the situation continued to develop in northern Virginia, it did not remain static elsewhere. The very first reports just after midnight on June 22 came from the south and west of Prince William, detailing road closures in Louisa County and shelters opening in Greene County.[171] Overnight in the mountainous terrain of the latter, rescue personnel focused on evacuating more than fifty-eight people in the Bacon Hollow area threatened by the floodwaters of the Roach River. Rains had made all the mountain roads in Greene County impassable, preventing rescue units from reaching some isolated areas, among them Shifflett Hollow and Mutton Hollow. Phone contact remained with the latter, and County Sheriff Harold T. Chapman believed the few people in Shifflett Hollow and other isolated areas would have no trouble reaching high ground. Opened as a shelter, Greene Elementary School housed sixty-eight people, supported by the Red Cross, with others choosing to stay with friends and relatives. In Madison County, immediately to the north, floodwaters from the Rose and Robinson

Rivers, tributaries of the Rapidan, isolated the mountain valley communities of Criglersville and Syria, and there too, mountain roads were impassable. Some residents evacuated voluntarily to county schools, and authorities moved children from the Graves Lodge Camp to spend the night at Madison High School. Although flooding was generally bad, the sheriff's department reported county buildings were open and there were no injuries or significant property damage.[172] Meanwhile, far to the south and west, in Rockbridge County, the rising Maury River led residents in low-lying areas of the city of Buena Vista to evacuate. Where the Maury met the James, it covered wide sections of the town of Glasgow.[173] Lynchburg witnessed the cresting of the James at twenty-six feet, which was four feet below the record set in 1771 but enough to flood areas of its waterfront, including Jefferson Street and the foundry of the Glamorgan Pipe & Foundry Company, necessitating the evacuation of fifty families and more than twenty businesses.[174]

Forty-two minutes into the new day, the City of Richmond activated its emergency operations center, and a little more than ten minutes later the Civil Air Patrol reported that by 8:30 a.m. it would have twenty-six aircraft, twenty mobile and thirty land stations available in affected areas. Meanwhile, the state highway department worked to confirm roadways that were open and available to expedite troop movements. Between 8:00 and 9:00 a.m., the first Coast Guard helicopter arrived at civil defense headquarters, the National Guard reported putting six men on duty in Scottsville to address looting as needed and the Red Cross was working to verify the situation in Prince William County. Virginia's civil defense apparatus was operating in high gear, and reports began to arrive indicating that things had stabilized in a number of areas. At 9:45 a.m., Amherst, Nelson, Albemarle and Madison Counties reported stable, as did Caroline County to the east and the Shenandoah Valley counties of Page, Shenandoah and Clarke. Aerial assessments of Culpeper and Loudoun Counties were underway.[175]

Although stability would spread in some regions of the state, for many of the communities of the Piedmont region, June 22 would be a day when they would have to gird themselves for the worst. As waters moved east from the Blue Ridge Mountains in the west to the fall line communities of the Piedmont's eastern boundary, they brought devastation with them. An example of this juxtaposition was the situation in the far south of the state where the Dan River crested at Danville at 4:00 a.m. Now, later in the day, some of the streets in Danville remained closed, but the city was nevertheless in recovery mode.[176] Just twenty-five miles to its northeast along the Dan River in Halifax County, however, the town of South Boston still awaited the floodwaters. When those waters did arrive later in the day, they covered a new bridge as well as the Riverdale section of the town. Floodwaters rose to the roofs of some warehouses and also inundated a small residential area and mobile home park, forcing evacuations.[177] The experience of South Boston was modest compared to what some other downriver communities, regardless of the amount of rain they had witnessed directly, faced as water from the west gathered and made its way east along the major river basins.

By 7:00 a.m., civil defense headquarters in Richmond was directing regional deputy coordinators to prepare for damage survey teams. At 9:45 a.m., the Soil and Water Conservation Service reported it had asked federal soil and agriculture conservation officials to assess damage in affected counties. Later, both the U.S. Department of Agriculture (USDA) and the U.S. Small Business Administration (SBA) requested flights around the state. After noon, the assistant supervisor for civil defense in the Department of Education asked all school superintendents to survey and report damage.

The attempt to promptly assess damage was understandable and consistent with the natural disaster assistance plan, and some local officials, like those in Albemarle County, asked that disaster analysis teams be sent. But it was also a source of consternation among those stretched to capacity by what they felt was still a continuing operational emergency. Donald Glenn, the Region I coordinator and thus a person whose portfolio included some of the communities hit the earliest, complained to headquarters just before noon on June 22 that some of the local officials were "very upset!!" when he contacted them to request that they fill out the prescribed forms. They did not, he relayed, believe they could get the information given the problems with which they were still dealing. In fact, some jurisdictions did not want damage survey teams dispatched at all.[178] An after-action evaluation of the Agnes response performance noted that "many" jurisdictions reported they had been contacted multiple times by different people asking for a damage assessment.[179] Similarly, in his after-action report, a Virginia official responsible in part for such survey teams remarked that after the experiences with both Camille and Agnes it was "obvious that survey teams cannot be put in the area to accumulate damage estimates quickly enough to satisfy the requirement for a declaration of state of emergency (disaster area) by either the Governor or the President." Since such declarations thus chose to rely instead on initial damage estimates provided by the state police, as well as those from regional or local civil defense coordinators, he recommended modification of the natural disaster assistance plan to reflect that reality.[180]

A little before 10:30 a.m., Virginia governor Linwood Holton made his own damage assessment survey. Holton had spent six hours the night before reviewing reports from around the state. According to one account, he believed that the new civil defense plan was working "excellently" and that all "that can be done to render state assistance is being done." He also reportedly heard repeatedly from state and local officials that despite the challenges they faced, the situation was nowhere near as bad as Camille had been in terms of loss of life and homes. Lifting off in a Virginia National Guard helicopter, the governor spent more than five hours touring flood-ravaged areas to see for himself, accompanied by Adjutant General of the Virginia National Guard William McCaddin, Civil Defense Coordinator Tom Credle, State Police Superintendent Harold Burgess and several members of the media.[181]

Flying low over Farmville, the governor reportedly whistled in amazement, exclaiming, "This place is really a mess."Aerial views west of Richmond along the James revealed inundation of all the low-lying areas astride the river. The Route 522 bridge at Maidens was still passable, but the buildings by the railway station were flooded. In Cartersville, ten miles west of Maidens as the crow flies, officials confirmed floodwaters had washed away an 844-foot-long wood and iron bridge on Route 45 earlier in the day. Dating from 1886, the bridge had withstood Camille but found Agnes to be too much. Soon two dozen swamped railroad coal cars appeared near the Bremo Bluff power plant. There a freight train had pulled in at about 8:00 p.m. on the night of Wednesday, June 21. With the James River rising rapidly at the time, the train engineer jumped off, leaving the engine still running; it continued to run until quenched by water rising around the cab.[182] Water had also inundated the large Virginia Electric Power Company (VEPCO) power plant at Bremo Bluff at 2:00 a.m. on the morning of June 22, forcing the evacuation of personnel by boat. When Camille came in 1969, a 41-foot-high levy around the plant protected it, but the waters of Agnes crested there at more than 45 feet, almost completely covering the forty-plus-year-old plant's generators and submerging the distribution substation serving the area. At 6:30 a.m., the transmission lines going into the plant were shut down.[183]

Governor Holton's helicopter landed briefly northwest of Scottsville on Route 6, where he took a cab to the water's edge on Harrison Street. Meeting with Mayor Raymond Thacker, whose funeral home in town was flooded, the governor asked what the town needed and pledged to make assistance available.[184] In the main streets of Scottsville's business district, virtually no one escaped the floodwaters: not the IGA store, the antique shop, the feed store, the hardware store, the dry goods store, the Dew Drop Inn, Skippy's Market, Coleman's Jefferson Shop, Bruce's Drug Store and Western Auto, not to mention others nearby, including the Uniroyal Rubber plant (where hundreds of people worked) and even a Scottsville school, where the cafeteria stood entirely submerged.[185]

The rains from Agnes, of course, had largely ended by the time the governor began exploring the state, but for many communities that did not mean the danger had passed. For some, this was in part because the rains continued for them. At the northern end of the Shenandoah Valley, for example, Agnes had already dumped more than six and a half inches in the Front Royal–Winchester area, and it continued to rain.[186] It would be 6:00 p.m. before the Shenandoah River crested at Front Royal at a level of twenty-eight feet, six feet above flood stage, but in the interim and after, the downstream effects were dramatic.[187] Shenandoah Farms, a subdivision straddling Warren and Clarke Counties and constructed close to the river, lost twelve houses dragged away by the floodwaters.[188] At least fifty families evacuated the area.[189] Throughout the day, rescue

Governor Linwood Holton on helicopter. *Courtesy* Richmond Times-Dispatch.

Above: Floodwaters at Bremo Bluff power plant. *Courtesy* Richmond-Times Dispatch.

Opposite, top: Route 522 bridge over the James River at Maidens. *Courtesy Library of Virginia.*

Opposite, bottom: Route 45 bridge over the James River at Cartersville covered by floodwaters. *Courtesy Library of Virginia.*

workers continued to operate. Intermittent telephone service caused by downed lines complicated their efforts, and at times responders found themselves driving as close to locations as they could and then finding it necessary to proceed by boat.[190] Meanwhile, in Clarke and Frederick Counties and the city of Winchester, volunteer firemen spent much of the day pumping water from hundreds of basements.[191] Amid the turmoil, a National Guard helicopter from Manassas landed at a shopping center in Front Royal to take Mabel Funk to a Charlottesville hospital. Funk, in an accident unrelated to the flood, fell off the roof of her home and ruptured her bladder.[192]

While continuing rain contributed to the remaining threats in the Shenandoah Valley, elsewhere it was not the rain but the gathering floodwaters from the west now heading east along river basins that posed the greatest danger. A little after 10:00 a.m., the Tidewater area reported to civil defense headquarters that it was not experiencing any problems. That would generally be the case throughout the disaster, as the region of Virginia's coastline largely escaped a direct hit from Agnes. But at the fall line on the western border of the Tidewater, danger lay ahead. Here, where rivers drop from the uplands of the Piedmont to the coastal plain, communities braced for the accumulating waters heading their way.

Fredericksburg on the Rappahannock River was one such fall line community. As early as 3:30 a.m., Fredericksburg officials requested assistance to evacuate families living near the banks of the Rappahannock, and the local National Guard commander reported mission authorization to provide forty men and ten trucks.[193] Ultimately, the Red Cross assisted some fifty families in Fredericksburg, housing some in the dormitories of what was then Mary Washington College.[194] At 8:45 a.m., Fredericksburg reported spotty flooding and the opening of shelters at the National Guard armory, some community buildings and at a fire department. Predicting that the Rappahannock would crest at 1:00 p.m., they worried about losing an old VEPCO dam. While the dam survived, on the night of Thursday, June 22, the Rappahannock crested at thirty-four feet above normal and almost reached the city's main downtown shopping area.[195]

Richmond officials also knew what might be in store for them at the fall line of the James, and so at 11:30 a.m. they requested a radio-equipped vehicle to take a team to Columbia to gather data to make a reasonable flood prediction for the state capital; the Civil Air Patrol obliged. It was a prescient move. Later that evening, at 7:19 p.m., the National Weather

Route 20 James River Bridge approach to Scottsville. *Courtesy Library of Virginia.*

Service reported that all its gauges along the James River were out—only the one at Columbia was believed to be exact.[196] Richmond would not be as fortunate as Fredericksburg.

Early on June 22, Richmond City officials, with the assistance of the Virginia Army National Guard, the Virginia Transit Company (which operated transit service in Richmond), the Virginia Red Cross and other volunteer organizations, initiated implementation of a flood-control plan, anticipating a crest of twenty-nine feet—twenty feet above flood stage and slightly above Camille—early the next morning. Concluding a meeting shortly before 1:30 a.m., city officials rushed to print a notice for distribution in likely flood areas. The document stated that there "is no protection whatsoever for persons and or property south of the James River. There is likewise no protection from James River flooding on the north side of the James River." Property owners who are exposed to the river, it urged, should "immediately take the steps necessary to either remove and or protect all persons and property from possible exposure to water from the James River." Officials advised businesses and residents in the Dock Street, Fulton and South Side areas to prepare for flooding worse than Camille.[197]

View of Scottsville from the James River Bridge. *Courtesy Library of Virginia.*

To protect the city as best as possible, work crews closed dikes and used a reported fifty thousand sandbags to increase the height of the dike along Dock Street, build a twenty-seven-foot-high bulwark around the vulnerable pumping station on Byrd Street and shore up other low-lying areas of South Side. After the city distributed the flyers to flood-prone areas early in the morning, police returned at 3:00 p.m. to encourage evacuation once more. Most businesses, apparently remembering Camille, chose to do so, moving their inventory throughout the day; many residents chose to wait. The city established two evacuation centers at local schools, and officials called more than 500 National Guard to duty at the Dove Street armory at 5:00 p.m. Midafternoon, city officials announced that all city offices would be closed the following day until 1:00 p.m., urging city businesses to do likewise; later, as a precautionary measure, they closed three of the city's bridges across the James that connect South Side Richmond to the rest of the city: the Boulevard, the Fourteenth Street and the old Ninth Street bridge; forty-five minutes later they also closed the Huguenot Bridge about six miles to the west. To avoid a repeat of some misfortune during Camille, VEPCO closed its Manchester substation and set up mobile substations. Between public works, utility and recreation and parks personnel, the city had some 850 people working on flood-control efforts, ultimately to be supplemented by almost 1,000 National Guardsmen. By the time darkness had descended, Richmond thus appeared as prepared for the approaching floodwaters as it could be.[198]

Conditions in northern Virginia continued to worry officials. Even relatively small streams in the region during Agnes would eventually greatly exceed their prior records for peak discharge (the rate of runoff, expressed in cubic feet per second, from a drainage area for a given rainfall). Goose Creek near Leesburg in Loudoun County would exceed it by twice as much, Difficult Run near Great Falls in Fairfax County by five times, Cedar Run near Catlett in Fauquier County by five and a half times, Cub Run near Centreville in Fairfax County by about sixteen times and Bull Run near Manassas in Prince William County by six times.[199] But still, chief among the fears at the time was concern over the Occoquan dam. Sometime between the late morning and early afternoon, the ninety-four-year-old one-lane bridge the town of Occoquan had fought so hard to save from demolition succumbed to the floodwaters coming over the dam.[200] So also did the filtration plant adjacent to the town, the raw water intake for the plant on the north bank of the river and the high service line that could be used to distribute water to Prince William County. As floodwaters inundated low-lying areas of the town along its main street, boats came unmoored from a riverside marina and floated into the river and through the streets of town, as did coffins from a flooded funeral home. At 4:30 p.m., reports arrived in civil defense headquarters noting that twenty-nine men from the Army Corps of Engineers at Fort Belvoir in Fairfax County had been sent to sandbag and reinforce the face of the Occoquan dam, over which ten feet of water still continued to flow. Some of these soldiers from the Eleventh Engineer Battalion had been working throughout the night installing boat bridges and rescuing stranded individuals in Fairfax County and Alexandria; now they worked on the Occoquan dam, assisted by local firemen and marines. State police at the Culpepper district reported that they had been told by officers on the scene that the dam could break "any minute."[201]

The Occoquan and Manassas areas were not the only parts of Prince William County in trouble. Unremarked on in reports to civil defense headquarters, other smaller tributaries of the Potomac had also been threatening life and property farther east and south in the county. Just a mile below the Occoquan River along US Route 1, small Marumsco Creek meandered through some neighborhoods and an army research facility before flowing into the Potomac. Swollen by Agnes late on the evening of June 21, it overflowed its banks, covering parts of US Route 1 and causing

Flooding of I-95 bridge in Richmond. *Courtesy Library of Virginia.*

the evacuation of a trailer park. Twenty-three-year-old Jerry Romans was attempting to make a delivery when floodwaters blocked the road. As he attempted to turn around in the parking lot of the abandoned trailer park, the water overtook him. Unable to swim, he climbed on top of his car and shouted for help, according to witnesses who heard the shouts but could not see him in the darkness. A few hours later, a little before 1:00 a.m., the waters receded and a local found Romans's lifeless body in the parking lot near the car.[202]

Another two miles south, another small waterway, Neabsco Creek, also crosses US Route 1, meandering peacefully on its way to the nearby Potomac River. Two vehicles mistook a flagman's wave as an instruction to

Ninety-four-year-old Occoquan bridge subsumed by floodwaters. *Courtesy Occoquan Historical Society.*

Ninety-four-year-old Occoquan bridge destroyed by floodwaters. *Courtesy Occoquan Historical Society.*

proceed across a bridge. Though both vehicles were swept away, onlookers rescued the occupants.[203] Five miles farther to the south, near Prince William County's southern border, Agnes threatened residents of Dumfries, the oldest continuously chartered town in the commonwealth. Quantico Creek here flows across US Route 1 as it makes its short journey east to the Potomac. Overflowing its banks with the Agnes rains, the floodwaters from the creek displaced residents along the adjoining Mine Road, a historic African American community formerly known as Batestown dating to the late eighteenth century. Members of the Dumfries-Triangle Fire Department traveled through the town assisting with evacuations, directing traffic, pumping out basements and otherwise aiding people in distress.

Soldiers sandbag the Occoquan dam. *Courtesy Library of Virginia.*

Councilman Wilmer Porter, flooded out of his own home, opened the town hall for his family and any who needed shelter.[204]

Despite what was happening in Occoquan and the eastern side of the county, it was conditions in Manassas in the west of the county that truly shocked some observers. Residents asserted that Bull Run, described as normally about twenty feet wide and only inches deep, had risen three feet an hour as both it and nearby Cub Run proceeded to bury the local neighborhoods of Sudley, Westgate, Loch Lomond and Yorkshire. Boats, according to one observer, were tied up to second-story windows and debris was everywhere. The sight of the devastation from the air spurred the governor to make an unscheduled stop during his initial helicopter tour of the flood damage. He landed near an elementary school, and after he and his team disembarked, a man approached, pleading for help. People were afraid of looters, he told the governor, and had no protection. After consulting with General McCaddin about what could be done and reboarding the helicopter, the governor remarked, "This is terrible." Landing moments later at the National Guard armory in Manassas, McCaddin ordered another 125 men into residential areas to prevent looting. Later that evening, after 10:00 p.m., Manassas requested portable lights for boats to aid in search and rescue and discourage looters.

Eventually, U.S. Marines as well as men of the 345th Company of Army Support Agency (ASA) Reserves from Philadelphia and New Jersey supplemented the Manassas contingent of guardsmen.[205]

Perhaps inevitably, false, inaccurate and incomplete reports continued to arise during the second day of emergency operations, particularly in the late afternoon and early evening hours. One Pentagon public information officer reported getting calls from citizens saying that a local radio station was broadcasting evacuation instructions for people in low-lying areas along the Potomac River without identifying any assembly points. A Civil Air Patrol mobile unit reported that a small aircraft had crashed into the James near Columbia. According to a Fluvanna County deputy sheriff, five or six witnesses said they saw the plane crash near the James River bridge, and eyewitnesses told the *Charlottesville Daily Progress* that a plane was flying "extremely low along the river and had to climb to get over the bridge." As it leveled out, according to the witness, "'it flipped over several times, then the fuel tanks seemed to explode. The pilot didn't have a chance.'"[206] No planes, however, were ever reported missing or overdue anywhere, and despite the alleged eyewitnesses, officials deemed the report false. Late in the afternoon, the Civil Air Patrol indicated a small plane was lost in the waters and appeared unoccupied near Rixeyville in Culpepper County. Local civil defense personnel subsequently confirmed that the report was unfounded; the plane was simply tied down and inundated by floodwaters from the Hazel River.[207] As if things were not bad enough in the Manassas area, around 9:00 p.m. a report arrived that the Lake Jackson dam outside Manassas was eroding, followed by a later report just after 10:00 p.m. that there was a six-foot break in the dam. Subsequent investigation determined by midnight that this was a false report; the dam was holding with some slight erosion reported after 1:00 a.m. as water ran over the emergency spillway.[208]

During and after his helicopter tour, Governor Holton was asked about a disaster declaration. Advised by officials that a disaster declaration the following day would be just as good, the governor insisted on having a more comprehensive understanding of the damage before asking the federal government for assistance. It was clear, however, that a declaration would come soon.[209] Accordingly, State Office of Civil Defense officials advised local governments that the state's disaster plan (COVANDAP) would likely be put into effect the next day. Through the office of James Hensley, the federal coordinating officer for the U.S. Civil Defense Preparedness Agency, officials notified U.S. First Army headquarters that Virginia would likely need their assistance, and later in the day, officials from the federal Office of Emergency Preparedness began to arrive in Richmond.[210]

The information for which the governor was waiting continued to come in throughout the day. In the late morning, Culpeper reported no deaths, injuries or missing persons but indicated it was now housing more than 200 people in the Federal Reserve Bank, Trailways buses and private homes. Mayor Parnell of Glasgow made a request for housing for 50 families. Warren County's civil defense coordinator and the county sheriff declared the county at the northern end of the Shenandoah Valley a disaster area. During the early evening hours, the Red Cross provided one of the first preliminary status reports on housing conditions in widespread areas of the state. In the southwest, in Pulaski County, 50 families were displaced and their homes damaged, while in Montgomery County 45 mobile homes had been destroyed. A little to the northeast, Roanoke, Salem, the town of Vinton and Botetourt and Craig Counties had at least 6 houses and 15 mobile homes destroyed, and 353 houses and more than 100 mobile homes

Water coming over the Occoquan dam on June 22. *Courtesy Library of Virginia.*

damaged; farther north Covington and nearby Valley Ridge had 134 houses with minor damage and 69 houses and 5 mobile homes with major damage; and farther north in the Shenandoah Valley's Augusta County, the city of Waynesboro had 100 people in shelters. Later in the evening the Red Cross handled a request from Fluvanna County's civil defense director for food, water, and milk for about 150 refugees. Surveys were still underway farther to the north in Spotsylvania, Stafford and Prince William Counties, as well as in the city of Fredericksburg.[211]

Water—to drink—became a growing problem. Both power plants and water treatment facilities in riverside communities suffered significant damage, in some cases jeopardizing the supply to areas far from the flooding. When the service main near the Occoquan dam ruptured, it left forty thousand residents in the Dale City area of Prince William County without water. But when the pumping stations near the town of Occoquan went out at about noon on June 22, this number jumped dramatically, cutting off the water supply to half a million people in northern Virginia. From the Occoquan area, civil defense headquarters received an urgent request for water treatment services, while at the same time Fairfax County reported that it had an alternative potable water source but needed containers for distribution. Around 9:30 p.m., the Fairfax County Water Authority, which operated the Occoquan dam and the water treatment facilities, requested several large industrial pumps. Along the James River in Rockbridge County, the same floodwaters that caused the evacuations in Glasgow also left the town without water.[212] Farther east along the James, in Fluvanna County, the postmaster at Bremo Bluff reported a power outage at 4:30 p.m. incapacitating pumps at the water treatment plant. And yet farther to the east on the river, Goochland County reported an outage that would cause storage tanks to run dry by the next day. The next morning requests related to drinking water needs would come from both the Dale City area of Prince William County and the city of Alexandria.[213]

In the south of the state, in Farmville, the water supply situation had been deteriorating for a while. As noted earlier, floodwaters forced closure of the water plant on the afternoon of Wednesday, June 21. By noon the following day, water was at the roof of the plant. To make the supply in storage tanks last as long as possible, the town asked residents to limit usage and requested that both industries and high water–using entities like laundries and local Longwood College close. The town manager remarked that it was "the most critical water situation we have had." With darkness falling Farmville reported to civil defense headquarters that sewage backup was exacerbating the water supply situation and pushing it to critical levels.[214]

As midnight approached on June 22, though worries about water availability remained, a relative calm descended over some areas that had experienced flooding. Earlier in the day there had finally been some good news out of northern Virginia when officials determined that the runaway barge on the Occoquan River had not done substantive damage to the I-95 bridge; officials reopened it to traffic at about 5:00 p.m.[215] A little before 11:30 p.m., the Culpepper Emergency Operations Center reported that it was closing down for the night, with the rivers not expected to rise more than eight inches and flooding not critical.[216] While these kinds of reports were no doubt welcome, in Richmond things were heading in the other direction.

JUNE 23

When looking at a map of Virginia, it is easy to imagine how near the Atlantic coast rivers flooded by days of heavy rains can slowly spread out over a wide delta or plain, relatively unconstrained and without the need to rise to threatening heights. But at the fall line, where the Piedmont area drops, sometimes precipitously, to the coastal plain, the rush of heavy rains accumulating from as far away as the mountain counties on the state's western edge can be intense. And Richmond sits at the fall line of the largest river basin in the state, the James.

Rains heavier than what drainage systems could accommodate had made roads scattered throughout Richmond impassable at times on June 22. But the floodwaters from the west that everyone feared began to arrive in the late hours of that day and the early hours of the next. At 12:30 a.m., the city added the I-95 bridge across the James to the earlier closures of the Huguenot, the Boulevard, the old Ninth Street and the Fourteenth Street bridges. The decision to close some bridges proved wise, as just after 1:30 a.m. on June 23, the National Guard confirmed that the Fourteenth Street bridge was underwater. Only the Lee Bridge and the new Ninth Street bridge remained open and the latter only for emergency traffic.[217]

To the later frustration of many, as it had in 1969 when Camille struck, water began leaking into the pumping station on Byrd Street, just west of Seventeenth Street, early on the evening of June 22, endangering the pumping equipment. Designed to keep the water level low behind the Shockoe Valley dikes, the pumps were an important part of the city's flood-control apparatus. When floodwaters during Camille caused cracks in the building that housed pumps, the forced abandonment of the pumps led to water backing up through the sewers behind the dikes and damaging part of Richmond's Main Street area. Once again, as with Camille, floodwaters leaking into the building forced a shutdown of the pumping operation and the station's abandonment by workers. Fifty National Guardsmen remained in the area to guard the dike and repair any leaks that might emerge if possible. At least one commentator later asserted that if the pumps had been able to be kept in operation, the flood level inside the city dikes could have been kept to about twenty-four feet. As it was, the National Guard reported high water at Broad and Seventeenth Streets as early as 2:20 a.m., and ultimately the water would rise to the second story of buildings in the business district of the Shockoe Valley.[218]

When advised early on June 22 to evacuate, one observer characterized the people in Shockoe Valley as "frenetic." Trucks loaded with goods and belongings tried to move out of the area while trucks filled with dirt to build up the dikes came in. Both struggled with traffic carrying sightseers looking to catch a glimpse of the rising James River. Fulton residents had been more skeptical, and in the early evening, the evacuation centers set up for them at the East End and Bainbridge Middle Schools were virtually empty. At around 10:00 p.m., however, attitudes started to change when three of the area's roads flooded. Eventually some four hundred residents of Fulton Bottom evacuated to shelters. Some, however, may have done so unnecessarily as a result of a false rumor. This particular rumor appears to be reflected in a Civil Air Patrol report to civil defense headquarters at 12:30 p.m. on June 23, asserting that there were three gas leaks, one in South Side and two near Fulton Bottom. According to the civil defense headquarters record, the Civil Air Patrol advised "possibility of explosion eminent [sic] and all aircraft advised to stay clear of area." There was, indeed, such a leak in the early afternoon of June 23, but National Guardsmen successfully patched it. With a rumor of a potential explosion spreading, however, some one hundred additional people evacuated their homes in response.[219]

Across the James River, in South Side there were relatively few residents left to worry about the levels of the river. After the devastating impact of Camille in 1969, most had decided not to rebuild and left, leaving the area to businesses, repair shops and oil company facilities. Of the residents who did remain, as well as the businesses and repair shops, most responded to

Top: Richmond's Fourteenth Street bridge underwater. *Courtesy Library of Virginia.*

Bottom: Floodwaters in Shockoe Bottom at Fifteenth and Main Streets in Richmond. *Courtesy Library of Virginia.*

city warnings by moving their goods and inventory to higher ground. But a different type of problem emerged near Commerce Road, home to fuel storage tanks for more than a dozen oil companies. Substantial flooding could float the large tanks off their foundations. In anticipation, refinery workers had spent Wednesday weighing the tanks down by filling them with fuel from tanks located on higher ground; where fuel was not available, firemen used water. By June 23, however, the floodwaters were indeed threatening the tanks. Water damaged areas between Hull, Commerce and Maury Streets in South Side, covering the railroad tracks and I-95 all the way to the loading platform for the Deepwater Terminal. Among the large facilities reportedly damaged were those of Standard Paper, Sampson Paint, Reynolds Metals, Miller Manufacturing, Moore's Building Supplies and Philip Morris. Most concerning, however, were five oil tanks, ranging from a couple hundred thousand gallons to four million gallons in capacity, which floodwaters had dislodged and tilted. According to company officials, if the tanks continued to rise and underwater connecting lines ruptured, there would be no way to prevent the oil in the tanks from draining into the river. The status of these tanks also became a subject of confused reports when at 1:10 p.m. an amateur radio operator informed civil defense headquarters that there was oil and gas in the water near Maury and Stockton Streets in South Side and that small tanks had turned over and large ones were floating; the information could not be confirmed.[220]

At 6:00 a.m., power went out in a portion of downtown Richmond, including the Capitol Square Complex. Civil defense headquarters received a report at 5:10 a.m. that three VEPCO men were missing. Headquarters deemed the report false, but water had in fact infiltrated VEPCO's station on Twelfth Street, and the company announced that little could be done until the waters receded. Richmond officials had city police and National Guardsmen cordon off the downtown area at 7:00 a.m., limiting access to essential services only, and a little over an hour later Governor Holton closed all state offices in the city and Mayor Bliley ordered the closure of city offices and all downtown offices and stores. As was occurring elsewhere in the state, water to drink now also became a potential issue for Richmond's inhabitants. Mayor Bliley, as well as the city's manager, William Leidinger, and utilities director, E.H. Lordley, were reportedly at the city's water treatment plant when at 8:00 a.m. floodwaters overflowed the impoundment basins and began inundating the pumps. Ordering employees out, they closed and abandoned the plant. A helicopter had to assist in evacuating thirty-five people.[221]

During their search for water-related resources, city officials found themselves reminded that other areas in the state were struggling as well. After receiving a direct request from Richmond for seventy-five water tanker trucks, the commanding general at the U.S. Army Quartermaster Center at Fort Lee contacted Thomas Credle, Virginia's coordinator for civil defense. Credle responded by suggesting the general inform the city's mayor that with a statewide need for water during the crisis, resources would need to be rationed and "that trucks will be made available as appropriate."[222]

A little before 3:00 p.m., President Nixon declared thirty-one counties in Virginia disaster areas, making entities there eligible for low-cost loans from the U.S. Small Business Administration. Unlocking the full scope of federal disaster assistance, however, depended on a request from the governor, and that reportedly came at 3:01 p.m. on June 23. After a morning helicopter review of the situation in the Richmond area, Governor Holton met with aides and officials by candlelight in a state capitol conference room bereft of electrical power and then signed a proclamation declaring an emergency to exist in sixty-three of Virginia's

Floodwaters in South Side Richmond. *Courtesy Library of Virginia.*

ninety-six counties and twenty-five of its thirty-eight cities. Following the proclamation, the governor addressed a letter to General George A. Lincoln, the director of the Office of Emergency Preparedness in the Executive Office of the President, noting that the damage from Agnes exceeded the capabilities of the state and local governments and formally requesting federal assistance under the Disaster Relief Act of 1970. The letter detailed the state's estimate of the toll attributable to Agnes thus far: deaths; damage or destruction of bridges; damage or destruction of more than 600 miles of primary and secondary roads, 3,100 homes and 600 businesses and industries; damage, disruption and destruction of major utilities; and damage to farms, farm equipment and crops. Officials estimated the cost of this damage at $160 million (equivalent to $1.2 billion in 2023), a figure deemed likely to rise as more information became available.[223]

Linwood Holton's emergency declaration and request fulfilled the formal requirements for obtaining federal assistance, thus enabling homeowners, businesses, public utilities and city and county governments

View of Richmond floodwaters from the I-95 bridge. *Courtesy Library of Virginia.*

Half the James River Bridge at Columbia, Virginia, wiped out. *Courtesy Library of Virginia.*

to qualify for a variety of federal grants and loans to repair, rehabilitate and rebuild. The Nixon Administration responded promptly, with General Lincoln calling the governor to relay that he had given instructions to expedite flood relief and "work out the red tape later." Responding to some apparent confusion, President Nixon later expanded his disaster declaration to cover all the areas identified by the governor and informed him that he would be naming the director of Region 3 of the Office of Emergency Preparedness, Francis X. Carney, as the federal coordinating officer to work with the state.[224] Governor Holton's actions also triggered formal operational implementation of the Commonwealth of Virginia Natural Disaster Assistance Relief Plan (COVANDAP), which committed 26 state agencies to 127 specific emergency responsibilities.[225]

In his remarks to the press after issuing the emergency proclamation, Governor Holton observed that the major problem in most areas was now drinking water, and throughout the remainder of the day reports arriving at civil defense headquarters reflected this challenge. At 4:00 p.m., the City of Alexandria in northern Virginia requested a 1,300-gallon-per-minute pump and hundreds of feet of coupling pipe, while nearby Fairfax County

Damage in Columbia, Virginia. *Courtesy Library of Virginia.*

reported receiving ten 400-gallon, four 1,000-gallon and three 750-gallon water tanks; Prince William County received four 5,000-gallon self-propelled tanks. Officials at the Richmond Flood Control Center reported at 6:45 p.m. that both the city and Henrico County would be out of water by 8:00 a.m. the following day; Mayor Bliley asked water-intensive businesses to close and advised the citizenry to limit use to drinking only. Firemen canvassed the city in the evening to encourage compliance.[226]

While a lack of power and shortage of water tankers hindered attempts to address the drinking water problem in Richmond, companies from elsewhere in the country attempted to fill the gap. The American Honda Motor Company in Gardena, California, for example, offered portable generators, trail machines and three-wheeled vehicles with floatation tires. Ralph Byers Tank Lines in New York offered milk tankers.[227]

Throughout most of the state, the floodwaters were now receding. In the west, river levels had run high, causing damage but falling short of record levels. As one moved east along those same rivers, however, floodwaters shattered records, some of long standing, hinting at the extent of the damage some communities faced. At Scottsville, the James crested at 34.02 feet on June 22, more than 3 feet above the record set in 1870; at Bremo Bluff, it crested more than 6 feet above its prior peak; at Columbia almost 4 feet higher; at Cartersville more than 4 feet higher; and at Richmond at 4:00 p.m. on June 23, the James rose to 36.51 feet, exceeding by 6 feet a record that had stood since 1771. Farmville, along the Appomattox River, experienced water levels more than 6 feet higher than a record set in 1940.[228] Thus, some communities still struggled with high waters even though they were now receding. At Columbia, for example, near where the Rivanna River intersects the James, dozens of residents found themselves still stranded at the eastern end of Main Street, and the community was effectively isolated from the outside, with access requiring either a motorboat that could navigate the floodwaters or a jeep that could manage a two-mile-long mud trail. The Red Cross provided relief by trucking emergency supplies in as far as possible and then taking them by boat down Main Street.[229]

Despite such travails, the worst finally did appear to be over. In addition to the receding waters throughout most of the state, a potential disaster was averted in the north. There, the U.S. Army Corps of Engineers determined that the Occoquan dam, a source of concern for two days, was no longer in danger, removing a threat to the town of Occoquan as well as to I-95 and U.S. Route 1.[230] With this improving news, however, came reminders of the costs borne as confirmed fatalities from June 21 and June 22 became known. Among those on the twenty-second were Allen Emanual Jones, who drowned driving across a flooded road in Prince William County, and Cecil Corgin O'Bannon, who drowned when his boat overturned in floodwaters in Fairfax County. Not far from civil defense headquarters, fifteen-year-old Timothy W. Arbuckle died when he fell into a hole between two gasoline storage tanks at a service station construction site; one of the tanks reportedly shifted, and he suffocated under the sand and water that poured in and covered him.[231]

4

RECOVERY AND ASSESSMENT

The sober tally of deaths associated with a natural disaster typically reflects only those caused directly by the event itself. With a disaster like Agnes, these would be the deaths attributable to the winds, floodwaters and associated debris that precipitate drownings or fatal physical trauma. Significant also, however, are the sometimes larger and more difficult to calculate indirect deaths resulting from a natural disaster's contribution to disease, malnutrition, dehydration, exposure, loss of income and other threats. It is a disaster's contribution to these latter types of deaths that disaster relief assistance largely aims to prevent. In the days after June 23, civil defense officials in Virginia, now with federal assistance, transitioned from addressing immediate dangers to mitigating the threats posed by what Agnes had left in its wake. For a time, they would have to deal with both simultaneously.

On Saturday, June 24, the day after issuing his emergency declaration, Governor Linwood Holton met at the state capitol with all agency heads and with officials from the president's Office of Emergency Preparedness.[232] With a disaster declared, federal assistance now began to flow to the state at a more rapid pace. From the earliest hours of the day, depending on the area of the state, officials navigated the transition from responding to immediate dangers to addressing threats that would arise in Agnes's aftermath. In some areas, notably Richmond and northern Virginia, emergency operations continued throughout the day, while elsewhere recovery and assessment began. But immediate dangers could emerge anywhere, and they did so intermittently.

Among the immediate dangers still requiring attention were the mostly receding, but still dangerously swollen and debris-laden, rivers in the state. Not long after midnight on Saturday, June 24, for example, there was a report of a barge fouled in the overhead power cables in the vicinity of the James River Light at Dutch Gap. This and another "runaway" barge and the potential danger they could cause would be a story throughout the day. The fouled vessel was a Southern Materials Sand and Gravel Company barge with a large fixed crane. After the barge broke loose, it became entangled in high-tension power lines in a cove near a VEPCO plant; the plant and lines were critical to providing power to Richmond. VEPCO requested a helicopter for observation and a boat strong enough to contain the barge.[233]

Dutch Gap is an area about ten miles south of Richmond. During the American Civil War, the Union army built a canal there to bypass a large oxbow in the James River. The resulting waterway ultimately became the main channel of the river. On June 23, the Coast Guard Fifth District Headquarters in Portsmouth sent the eighteen-month-old, 157-foot-long buoy tender *Red Cedar* upriver to Hopewell to perform search and rescue and to try to keep the channel of the James free of debris. Given the power of the swollen river, *Red Cedar* reportedly ran at full speed against the current just to make three knots. Early in the moonlit hours of June 24, officials dispatched *Red Cedar* to secure the sand and gravel barge at Dutch Gap. On arriving, the crew of the vessel found it difficult to anchor given the current and had to repeatedly use their engines to stay on station. On further investigation, the captain found he could not enter the cove or reach the barge with a tow line, forcing him to abandon the effort. Ultimately, at 3:30 p.m., a tugboat arrived and freed the barge, while *Red Cedar* remained on station in the area.[234]

The Southern Materials barge was not the only one to draw attention on June 24. At noon, the Civil Air Patrol reported a barge "rapidly approaching the Ben Harrison Bridge across the James River at Hopewell." About fifty minutes later, the State Highway Department reported that a tugboat was in pursuit of the barge and that the Civil Air Patrol and the Coast Guard would try to coordinate. The only problem with the reports was that no such barge was discovered. Although around 8:30 p.m. the Coast Guard observed a sixteen-by-ten-foot wooden raft, which they recovered and moored to the bank, after conducting a broader search they could not locate any barge. They ultimately concluded that the wooden raft must have been what the Civil Air Patrol observed.[235]

Debris colliding into facilities downriver was one potential danger for communities otherwise unaffected by Agnes, but after June 23, there was still one large community in danger of flooding. Late on June 23, the National Weather Service issued a bulletin predicting record-breaking floods for Petersburg, with the Appomattox River expected to crest at forty feet.[236] Situated along that river about ten miles before it empties into the James and about thirty miles south of Richmond, the city of Petersburg was home to about thirty-six thousand people. Because the waters of the Appomattox generally moved slower than those of the James, residents anticipated that it would crest there later than in other locations. The city had prepared accordingly, with the National Guard armory preparing to shelter refugees, police alert to the potential for looting, residents advised of the potential danger by door-to-door contact and elderly residents who might need assistance identified in advance. Officials also established a plan for the potential evacuation of Pocahontas Island, which had been the home of a large free Black population stretching back to the days just after the American Revolution.[237]

As late as June 26, authorities continued to worry about the cresting Appomattox at Petersburg. In what was a happy outcome in relative terms, such fears turned out to be exaggerated. The *Petersburg Progress-Index* reported on Sunday, June 26, that the "expected flood in this city has been greatly downgraded"; the river ultimately crested with little disruption. A number of factors contributed to the city's good fortune. Rain in the area was lighter than it had been in Farmville and to the west. Additionally, a large flat area between Farmville and the Appomattox River's Brasfield Dam absorbed a great deal of water in creeks and adjoining swamp land. Last, the slow flow of the Appomattox allowed rainfall in the Petersburg area to dissipate before the floodwaters from the west arrived. A city public works official pointed out that they had been fooled. When the Appomattox flooded the city in 1940, he noted, the swamps that adjoin much of the river were full after heavy rains. This time, luckily, the swamps were dry, and the waters of the swollen river were able to spread out along its long, flat journey toward the Atlantic.[238] Everywhere in the state now, waters were receding, and renewed flooding was no longer a concern.

The prospect of looting, in contrast, remained a source of anxiety. Two days earlier on the evening of June 22, eight residents of a flooded northern Virginia trailer park near Manassas, unsatisfied with the protection being provided, reportedly armed themselves with shotguns and ordered everyone out of the area.[239] On Saturday, June 24, requests came to civil defense headquarters throughout the day for the dispatch of National Guardsmen. A little after 9:00 a.m., Henrico County requested thirty guardsmen; in the early

Above: Bridge section drifting in Nelson County. *Courtesy Library of Virginia.*

Opposite: Coast Guard vessel *Red Cedar*. *Courtesy Defense Visual Information Distribution Service.*

afternoon, Farmville requested sixteen in addition to those already stationed there. During the early evening, Columbia also requested guardsmen. It was not always clear if the requests for guardsmen were in response to concerns over looting or for other purposes, however. Columbia's request specifically cited looting concerns, and two days later, the National Guard in Manassas in northern Virginia requested state police assistance to address looting.[240]

Flood-borne disease was a concern as well as a source of wide disagreement. In addition to the general runoff that included debris, animal carcasses, fertilizer and other elements, sewage plants affected by Agnes had become inundated, and though the facilities were shut down or bypassed, their effluent often discharged into the floodwaters. But with the possible exception of people wading or playing in sewage that had backed up into urban streets, effluent from plants apparently did not pose a significant risk. In Henrico County, for example, the utilities director noted on June 23 that although most of the county sewage was now going into the James River, it was so diluted by floodwaters that it did not pose a general health hazard (although the health director did advise those on wells to boil their water).[241]

Nevertheless, when it came to what action, if any, to take after exposure to floodwaters, there was significant disagreement between local and state health officials. On their own initiative, a number of local health departments made requests for tetanus and typhoid vaccines. In Farmville, for example, the Prince Edward County Health Department placed orders for typhoid vaccines while the flooding was still going on, announcing that it would vaccinate everyone exposed to floodwaters against typhoid fever. By June 25, officials there reported that they had inoculated four hundred people. Alexandria also reportedly received typhoid and tetanus serums.[242] Fairfax County's health department offered free tetanus and typhoid shots at three different locations.[243] The health department director in Prince William County reported they had vaccinated at least three thousand people in the county by Monday, June 26; in fact, in Prince William County, officials required all rescue workers who had been in or near floodwaters be inoculated.[244]

Tetanus shots were not a problem, but administration of typhoid vaccines was a different matter. As the requests for typhoid serum came in from a growing number of local health departments, state officials reminded them of both the Virginia and U.S. Public Health Service's policy on its use. Neither recommended it in these circumstances. When reminded, the head of Fairfax County's health department responded that he wanted to have some on hand in the event he was "pressured into using it."[245] Richmond's director of the city health department, Dr. Freeman C. Hays, explained to the press that the idea of giving typhoid vaccines was discussed after Camille but determined to be unnecessary and was still considered so. When critics retorted that the police and National Guard were warning people to stay away from the floodwaters due to the risk of contracting typhoid, Dr. Hays responded that they were not doing so on his authority and were warning people for the wrong reasons. The governor's admonishment to stay out of floodwaters, he asserted, was for reasons of general safety, not due to disease risk.[246] Despite the state and federal positions on the use of the vaccine, before U.S. Small Business Administration personnel would go into the field on June 26, they insisted on receiving typhoid shots. Virginia's state health department instructed them to come to the health department at 9:00 a.m. on June 25, where the state epidemiologist would administer their shots.[247]

In contrast to the disagreement about the health threat posed by exposure to floodwaters, everyone agreed that in some areas the drinking water situation was critical. Henrico County officials, for example, though not particularly concerned about sewage effluent, recognized that for a time their fresh water supply was limited. Accordingly, the county's Board of Supervisors voted unanimously to prohibit nonessential business uses, threatening to cut off the water of those who did not comply.[248] Although concern about access to drinking water would be a focus over subsequent days, in many of the areas struck by Agnes, even those especially hard-hit, water treatment plants were unaffected. Where floodwaters rendered the plants inoperable, officials in a number of cases could bypass affected facilities, draw from storage tanks or connect to other systems to keep potable water flowing. Despite the concerns expressed about the water supply at Farmville on June 22, for example, the river's floodwaters did not reach the water plant's filter system, nor was the clear water well of some 100,000 gallons substantively affected. Although the plant was not able to begin operating again until late on June 25, with the exception of some of those living on high ground, water from storage tanks continued to flow to most residents.[249] By June 24, with the exception of what turned out to be unwarranted fears regarding the Appomattox River cresting at Petersburg, the only areas still considered critical in the state were Richmond and northern Virginia.[250] For both, the issue remained potable water.

In Richmond, floodwaters were not expected to recede until June 26, and some one thousand National Guardsmen had been brought in to supplement police guarding various locations.[251] On June 23, officials tested four artesian springs and found them safe for public use. While the springs offered a valuable source of water, the means by which to get water to the populace nevertheless posed a problem. Officials believed they would need seventy-five tankers with a capacity of five thousand gallons each to distribute water from mobile treatment units and from more than twenty fire stations. This was a significant logistical challenge given the need for tankers elsewhere in the state and, as remarked on earlier, generated a testy reply from Coordinator Credle when the city made an independent request to the army for tankers. Other entities, however, did offer support, with Lone Star Industry in Dinwiddie, two counties to the south, donating forty-five thousand gallons for use south of the James. (It was ready to supply farther north in Richmond but could not get across the James River.)[252] The Air Force also flew in twenty-two three-hundred-gallon collapsible portable water tanks that could be used to replace tanker trucks, which in turn could then be sent out to bring in water from other locations.[253]

Preparing for the expected exhaustion of water in the city's reservoirs early that evening, on June 24 officials opened water stations throughout the city and in parts of adjacent Henrico County.[254] There was little demand.[255] That changed after 6:00 p.m. when Richmond's reservoirs ran dry, as did the

Floodwaters in Richmond. *Courtesy Library of Virginia.*

spigots of some 100,000 people. Those affected consisted of city residents
north of the James and west of Seventeenth Street and some 85 percent of
the residents of Henrico County.[256] In a turnabout of fate, the residents of
heavily flooded South Richmond were unaffected. They would continue to
receive fresh, drinkable water from Chesterfield County to the south, where
there was no water crisis and where a slowly rising Appomattox River would
not create one.[257]

Once water stopped flowing from spigots, the thus far little-used Richmond
water stations experienced a sharp rise in patronage.[258] A shortage of
portable containers plagued efforts from the start. Officials asked residents
to bring their own containers, if possible, which resulted in the creative use
of a wide variety of household containers; one elderly woman reportedly
arrived with several empty gallon-sized bourbon bottles.[259] Eventually,
the city ordered twenty thousand containers from civil defense officials.[260]
Richmond officials limited water usage to cooking and drinking use only and
asked businesses and industries that required water for any purpose other
than sanitation to close. Henrico County agreed to cooperate with the city's

restrictions.[261] With use limitations now firmly in place, one reporter implied some might view a cleanly shaven face as the public mark of a scofflaw.[262]

A modest piece of good news emerged when inspections of Richmond's water treatment plant found that floodwaters had caused little damage to either the plant's electrical system or its physical structures. This prompted the city's utility director, H.E. Lordley, to propose an interim measure to restore some water service as soon as possible.[263] As a result, on the evening of Sunday, June 25—a little more than twenty-four hours after the spigots had gone dry—Richmond began pumping water again at a rate of forty million gallons a day.[264] Lordley's interim measure accommodated a treatment plant whose filters were still covered by floodwaters, forcing abandonment of one of the three components of the normal water purification process. Limited to the remaining purification steps of coagulation (the creation of larger and heavier particles in the water that then settle to the bottom of tanks) and chlorination alone, operators used ten times the normal amount of chlorine to kill parasites, bacteria and viruses.[265] While a welcome advance toward normalcy, the resulting unfiltered water was not for drinking but limited to sanitary (e.g., toilet) and fire protection needs alone; in fact, officials advised

Floodwaters in Richmond. *Courtesy Library of Virginia.*

residents not to use the water for bathing or even for showering if a person had breaks in the skin. City officials also stressed that the water was not to be used for commercial purposes or for cleaning flooded areas.[266]

Not everyone complied with the restrictions, and by the late afternoon of June 26, Richmond officials had cut off water to the sites of thirty-five violators, including multiple businesses, residences and apartment complexes.[267] To assist in the rationing of water, both the governor and the mayor closed most state and city offices in Richmond.[268] By 8:30 a.m. on Thursday, June 29, normal water operations had resumed in Richmond, a little more than four and a half days after the spigots had gone dry (normal service resumed in Henrico County twelve hours later). During the most critical moments of the water shortage, according to the director of general services in Richmond, the city used twenty five-thousand-gallon tankers, fifteen one-thousand-gallon tankers and twelve four-hundred-gallon tankers provided by the U.S. Army, as well as tankers from Dairymen Inc. and other civilian sources; some came from as far away as Philadelphia.[269] A regional effort had ensured that residents of Richmond had the water necessary.

Northern Virginia was the other area of the state still considered in critical condition on June 24. There, on June 22, the Agnes-induced floodwaters of the Occoquan River had rendered inoperable the two water filtration plants that straddled the river in Prince William and Fairfax Counties and later destroyed the thirty-six-inch water main that crossed the river and supplied eastern Prince William County. Together the two stations provided up to fifty million gallons of water daily to a total of almost half a million people.[270] With the disruption, authorities declared a water crisis in Fairfax County, the city of Alexandria and parts of Prince William County. Some in all three areas were without water, while others drew from a two-day reserve in storage. Officials, accordingly, asked residents to limit their usage to drinking, cooking and sanitary needs only, while ordering beauty shops, laundries and other large commercial users of water to close.[271] In the Dumfries and Triangle areas of Prince William County, residents benefited from an emergency hookup with nearby Marine Base Quantico; in other areas, officials established water pick-up locations at fire stations, pools, schools and civic centers.[272]

Given the demand for tankers and pumps throughout the areas affected by Agnes, the state could not fill the need in northern Virginia, so localities there had to look elsewhere for assistance. Fairfax County picked up four pumps from Mechanicsburg, Pennsylvania, and garnered some 1,000-gallon, 750-gallon and 400-gallon tankers from the U.S. Army base at Fort Belvoir.[273]

Ultimately, Fairfax received and deployed twenty large water tanker trucks to areas with low water supply, while also drawing 15 million gallons of water a day from the District of Columbia, Arlington County and the cities of Fairfax and Falls Church. To accommodate the limited supplies, officials in Fairfax asked residents to cut their water use by two-thirds until repairs could restart the pumping of water from the Occoquan reservoir.[274] Meanwhile, Prince William County also had a need for tanker trucks. Camp Pickett, a Virginia Army National Guard installation more than one hundred miles to the south, had sent northward four 5,000-gallon trucks originally destined for Fort Belvoir and Fairfax County. Officials diverted these for use in Prince William instead.[275]

As in Richmond, operators of the Occoquan water treatment plants moved quickly to implement interim measures and rush repairs as soon as receding floodwaters allowed. In one instance, floodwaters at the smaller plant adjacent to the town of Occoquan left a pump intact, though inoperable, while reducing to rubble the building holding the pump's electrical fittings.[276] Firefighters from both Prince William and Fairfax assisted in pumping an estimated 360,000 gallons of floodwaters out of the buildings' housing equipment.[277] Thanks to the efforts of the firefighters and water authority personnel, about 75 percent of whom worked almost around the clock beginning on the evening of June 21 when the floodwaters first looked to threaten the plants, by June 24 water again began to flow. Awaiting the arrival of pipe to replace the damaged thirty-six-inch transmission main, the smaller plant next to the town began pumping water directly to Prince William users at a rate of 9 million gallons a day. Meanwhile, the plant on the north side of the river began limited pumping of water to areas north of Occoquan. Together the two plants on June 24 were providing 60 to 75 percent of the water available during normal operations. Noting that it takes 3 to 4 million gallons of water just to fill the lines, authorities asked residents to continue curtailing use for a few days so that pressure could build up in the system sufficient to reach higher areas.[278] The water crisis in northern Virginia was over.

In addition to providing access to potable water, restoring electrical power was another priority in the post-disaster recovery process. Floodwaters had inundated a number of VEPCO plants, most dramatically the large Bremo Bluff plant along the northern bank of the James River in Fluvanna County. VEPCO officials estimated that both the Bremo Bluff Station, as well as the flooded Twelfth Street Station in Richmond, would be out of service for four or five months and had sustained damages amounting to at least $3.5 million ($25.8 million in 2023 dollars).[279] To address the situation in the interim, VEPCO installed a temporary transformer to the extant power lines at Bremo Bluff, restoring power to Fluvanna County on June 24 and to the entirety of Richmond two days later.[280] But with the Bremo Bluff and Twelfth Street Station plants out of commission, VEPCO faced reduced reserve capacity, and the fear of potential blackouts from excessive demand persisted throughout the summer.

With the issues of public safety, potable water and electrical power largely resolved by June 25, recovery and assessment efforts began in earnest throughout the state, with an emphasis on cleanup, assistance to affected individuals and businesses and collection of more reliable damage assessments. The chronological account from civil defense headquarters reflects this transition. Record entries dropped dramatically to approximately a dozen or less in subsequent days. At 11:25 p.m. on June 29, the emergency operations record reflects that answering services would take over at midnight.[281] The transition to recovery and assessment had taken place.

In those areas struck earliest by Agnes, cleanup efforts began days ahead of those still in the path of the floodwaters making their way eastward along the state's major river basins. Farthest south, adjacent to the North Carolina border, the hardest-hit areas in Danville were almost entirely clear of water by June 23. Stores were open or soon to open as the waters of the Dan River continued to recede.[282] It would take longer in South Boston farther east along the Dan, where the Route 58 and Route 501 intersection in the Riverdale section of town remained under three feet of water and the river did not begin receding until about 10:00 p.m.[283] Early hit areas in the west also were among the first to begin clearing away the detritus of the storm. As early as June 23, most of the people along the Tye, Piney and Rockfish Rivers in Nelson County returned to their homes, as did those in Glasgow in adjacent Rockbridge County.[284] In Waynesboro, just to the north in Augusta County, where the state had set up one of five packaged disaster hospitals on June 24, stores reopened on the same day and found themselves again flooded, this time with bargain shoppers perusing sales on flood-damaged items.[285] A similar flood of some five thousand shoppers besieged the fairgrounds at Fredericksburg a few days later to check out a sale of damaged items from J.C. Penney.[286]

As floodwaters receded throughout the state, cleanup efforts expanded. Residents, business owners, industry employees, local government personnel and volunteers all contributed to the effort, beginning the long, discouraging process of salvaging personal items and business inventory as best they could, clearing debris and shoveling and washing mud off flooded streets and out of inundated buildings. The public works department in Prince William County collected debris in the western part of the county, while the Occoquan-Woodbridge Sanitary District handled the job in much of the east.[287] In Occoquan, shops in the heart of the small town suffered damage from multiple sources: streams overflowing and rushing down the town streets to the river, underground stormwater systems bursting through their grates and the Occoquan River rising up from the north. During the flooding, a reported 150 boats escaped the confines of Prince William Marina in the town's business area, some floating out into the town streets to bang against or lodge themselves among the shops and restaurants. County Supervisor Vernon Dawson, who owned a restaurant, part of a funeral home and another building he was renovating on the town's main street, saw all three suffer serious damage or be washed away. Asked what he planned to do as he helped direct volunteers, Dawson was unsure but reportedly smiled and responded, "Just say I'm at the 10-yard-line and going to punt.'"[288]

Aerial view of floodwaters in Occoquan. *Courtesy Occoquan Historical Society.*

Volunteers were a critical component of the cleanup effort in Occoquan. Among the earliest were the members and the Ladies Auxiliary of VFW Post 7916, whose building sat high enough to avoid the floodwaters. On the morning of Thursday, June 22, they assisted firemen and sheriff's deputies in directing traffic and helped townspeople salvage their effects. The next day, they set up a small canteen offering coffee and doughnuts to members of the National Guard, U.S. Army and other branches of the military who had begun arriving in Occoquan late in the morning the day before. On Saturday, June 25, the Salvation Army arrived to assist but, after observing the VFW in action, asked post commander Ed Bedron if he would be willing to continue the post's good work while they left to assist others who had no such help. Agreeing to the arrangement, another officer of the post, Don Totman, then started calling around the area for food donations, which soon resulted in a plethora of sandwiches, soup and other food that the post made available to everyone. After VFW Post 7916 offered to billet the National Guardsmen in Occoquan, other VFW posts donated blankets and supplies.[289]

Other volunteers also assisted in Occoquan. As early as the evening of Wednesday, June 21, Boy Scouts Explorer First Aid Post 1364 worked with volunteer firemen and others who sheltered refugees at the Botts Fire Station. Now, after the crisis had passed, Explorer members pitched in to help clean up the town.[290] On Saturday, June 25, Ed Jones, the president of the civic association in the nearby Lake Ridge community, asked Occoquan mayor Robert Ritenour what could be done to assist the town. Ritenour reportedly said he needed strong men to help with cleanup. After knocking on doors in Lake Ridge, Jones reportedly returned with somewhere between seventy and one hundred men, women and teenagers, who quickly got to work.[291]

Many communities in Virginia, in fact, benefited from the contributions of volunteers during the recovery effort. In Scottsville, for example, the mayor asserted that assistance from University of Virginia students meant cleanup efforts were six to ten days ahead of what they had been during Camille.[292] Once again volunteers from Mennonite churches assisted, traveling to Richmond, for example, to help with cleanup in Fulton.[293] Meanwhile, jurisdictions also attempted to help one another. The Charlottesville public works department, for instance, aided Scottsville, Waynesboro and Richmond.[294]

But the source of labor and support for such efforts did, at times, generate tension. When Camille struck in 1969, then governor Mills E. Godwin Jr.

Lake Ridge volunteers arrive in Occoquan. *Courtesy Occoquan Historical Society.*

Clearing debris in Columbia. *Courtesy Library of Virginia.*

found himself navigating a difficult public relations misunderstanding when he allegedly refused National Guard help for Scottsville. In reality, the situation arose because the local civil defense commander was already finding it difficult to manage the volunteers in the Scottsville-Howardsville area. While the Mennonite volunteers worked diligently, he noted, other "volunteers" were mere sightseers or worse, looters, creating significant discipline problems. As a result, he put out the word that the area needed no more assistance. Meanwhile, local guardsmen had offered to volunteer and, apparently not knowing the background, reacted negatively when their request was denied.[295]

With Agnes it appeared that some localities sought to use National Guard troops for cleanup duties, contrary to state policy. While the situation was still critical in some areas on June 23, General McCaddin of the Virginia National Guard, rather forcefully it appears, and with the approval of the governor, reminded everyone that localities had an obligation to deploy their own resources for cleanup duty. National Guard troops, he noted in a message, would "not be assigned to any area for the purpose of debris removal or cleanup. This is a Policy Statement!!" (emphasis in original), reads the entry in civil defense headquarters records. "Upon declaration by the President, localities can contract for cleanup and upon completion of the work with proper documentation can be eligible for a project grant."[296] What served as the catalyst for this announcement is unclear, but on June 24 the press reported that the National Guard was working with volunteers to clean up Farmville.[297] That same day, Farmville requested sixteen additional guardsmen, as well as an extension of tours to June 25 of those already there—a request officials granted.[298] In contrast, however, less than five hours later authorities denied a request from the Roanoke Salem area. This latter request asked that National Guard troops there serve their two-week summer training in the area.[299] It seems likely that the Roanoke Salem request was seen as an attempt to rope local guardsmen, probably with their concurrence, into flood cleanup duty. This would certainly be consistent with what occurred just a day later, when members of the 6th Battalion of the 111th Artillery in Manassas signed a petition, routed to Richmond via the chamber of commerce, asserting that their time would be better spent on local flood cleanup than in their annual two-week summer training scheduled for Camp Drum, New York. Officials from Warren County made a similar request through their delegate to the Virginia General Assembly. A spokesman for the governor responded that the governor had been "unequivocal" in a meeting on June 24 with state agency leaders when he asserted that the work of the National Guard was protection of life and property, "We're not in the cleanup business," he reportedly stated, "and we're not going to go into it."[300] Soon after, National Guard operations began closing down. Guardsmen in Manassas and Occoquan, for example, were scheduled for release at 6:00 p.m. on June 26 and 8:00 a.m. on June 27, respectively. At 8:30 p.m. on June 26, the National Guard liaison in Richmond closed his station.[301]

By June 24, the state health department had set up packaged disaster hospitals in Amherst, Waynesboro and Clifton Forge, as well as two in Prince William County.[302] With the declaration of disaster areas by President Nixon, officials could now also open offices that provided federal financial aid to businesses and individuals. On June 25, Governor Holton met in Harrisburg, Pennsylvania, with the governors of four other mid-Atlantic states affected by Agnes. There, George Lincoln, director of the president's Office of Emergency Preparedness, assured the attendees that federal help was on its way.[303] Two days later, the government opened a Federal Disaster Assistance Center in Richmond, and while Vice President Agnew visited Richmond for two hours the very next day, the government opened similar centers in Alexandria, Covington, Fredericksburg, Lynchburg, Manassas, Salem, Scottsville and Waynesboro.[304]

Under the Federal Disaster Relief Act of 1970, these offices purported to offer a single location where those affected by a natural disaster could get help in obtaining all the federal and state assistance authorized by law, sometimes within as soon as a week of applying, from agencies like the U.S. Small Business Administration (SBA), Department of Housing and Urban Development (HUD), Department of Agriculture (USDA) and Virginia's Employment Commission. Most critical to many, relief included free temporary housing for up to a year and, for those with housing financed through Veterans Administration loans, forbearance on mortgage payments. Virtually any non-governmental organization with tangible property losses from flooding could apply for assistance from the SBA to restore their property to as near pre-disaster levels as possible. This assistance took the form of variable rate loans (then at 5.125 percent) for a term of up to thirty years and in amounts of up to $500,000 for businesses, $50,000 for homes and $10,000 for personal property (or a combined $55,000 for homes and personal property). Local officials stressed the need to keep detailed records to receive reimbursement from federal funds for damage expenses. Also available were food coupons, as well as unemployment compensation up to the maximums allowed by Virginia's unemployment program. For those who applied by July 26, the latter provided anywhere from $47 to $59 a week for up to twenty-six weeks. Farmers too could receive additional specific benefits that included grants for livestock feed, cost-sharing for repairs and the restoration of farmland, tax credits for replacement of certain equipment and buildings and emergency permits for grazing. For state and local governments, federal assistance provided up to 50 percent of the cost of repairing or replacing infrastructure and utilities, as well as limited indemnification through federal grants for lost property tax revenue due to floods.[305] Among the early flood relief checks was one presented by the national administrator of the SBA to the chair of Standard Paper Manufacturing Company. Totaling $753,000, the check covered a direct loan of $500,000 and the balance due on an earlier disaster loan related to Camille.[306] By early July, more modest-sized relief checks were arriving for affected families and businesses all over the state. Local newspapers often posted a photograph of a government official handing the check over to the recipients.[307] Some of these recipients would also find themselves in the uncomfortable position of receiving new loans while still paying off those associated with Camille, which would ultimately lead the SBA to suspend repayment of loans related to Camille (80 percent of the recipients of which were also affected by Agnes) until the beginning of 1973.[308]

Unfortunately, one type of relief far too many would not see was an insurance payment. Almost all property and business private insurance policies at the time excluded flood damage, but the National Flood Insurance Act of 1968 had created the National Flood Insurance Program (NFIP) precisely to fill this gap. Offering heavily subsidized coverage, eligibility for businesses and individuals depended on localities adopting certain land use and flood protection regulations. Even where jurisdictions had adopted the requisite regulations and secured eligibility for the program, however, few Virginia businesses and individuals had purchased the insurance. In the metropolitan D.C. area, an insurance association executive estimated that probably less than 10 percent of the heavy losses in the area would be recovered because of the low participation rate. Arlington County, Fairfax County and the cities of Fairfax and Alexandria in northern Virginia all qualified for NFIP. There were, however, only 177 policyholders in all of northern Virginia, and 71 of those were for homes in the Arlandria section of Alexandria.[309]

Some of the most heavily damaged areas in Virginia had never even sought eligibility. In Prince William County, for example, where both the commercial businesses in the east and residential areas in the west were among the hardest hit in the state, no one had flood insurance—in part because the county had never applied to qualify for eligibility. A few weeks after Agnes, officials reported that the Prince William County attorney was trying to determine what the county needed to do to participate in the national flood insurance program.[310]

But northern Virginia was not the only area of the state where people apparently paid scant attention to the protection offered by NFIP. Henrico County qualified in December 1971, but by the time Agnes arrived there were only seven policies in place there. Only three more existed in Northampton County. Some towns and cities, including Waynesboro, had been eligible but failed to comply with additional regulations by the end of 1971 and were dropped from the program.[311] When Camille struck Scottsville in 1969, a county official reported that no town merchants had flood insurance. Despite the damage from Camille, however, it appeared many still did not when Agnes arrived almost three years later. One Scottsville merchant, questioned about insurance by a reporter who followed the governor on his June 22 tour of the state, responded that it was "too expensive." He urged the reporter to tell people in the state what happened in Scottsville because "'we never heard from the federal or state government about their flood insurance.'"[312] Overall, according to one analysis, of the 77 flood-prone areas in the state, only 14 had applied for and secured approval to participate in NFIP, and in those only 621 homeowners and businesses had bought the insurance.[313]

Richmond was among the jurisdictions that had not even applied for eligibility. Allegedly, city officials—among the most vociferous the city attorney—opposed entry into the program because they believed a restrictive floodplain ordinance would render areas on either side of the James River unattractive to industries and businesses. Some objected to the fact that it was not available for property owned by the city. Others believed small businesses in the floodplain would not qualify because of high profits, or mistakenly thought only family dwellings could obtain coverage and that those under the ownership of the Richmond Redevelopment and Housing Authority (RRHA) in Fulton Bottom were ineligible. That NFIP flood insurance availability would somehow increase the city's liability was another concern. The city had faced lawsuits from some sixty plaintiffs after Camille, winning two and settling others. After the city's insurers paid out $350,000 to settle the claims (the city paid $100,000 itself), the insurer canceled the city's policy.[314]

Public criticism of the city on the issue of flood insurance after Agnes was almost immediate. When Vice President Agnew visited Richmond on

June 28, he expressed a desire to meet flood victims, and officials charged city police with locating some. Asked what they were going to say to the vice president, one of the victims reportedly responded, "We want flood insurance." Both he and a companion claimed to be angry that the city never qualified for coverage after Camille.[315] A subsequent study prepared by academics at Virginia Commonwealth University for the Central Richmond Association half a year later concluded that had Richmond qualified for the national flood insurance program before Agnes, approximately 82 percent of the businesses and almost all the homes would have been able to obtain insurance that would have covered all their direct losses. No action was anticipated in the near future, however, as the city now faced eighty damage claims related to Agnes.[316]

Debates about flood control projects and restricting floodplain development would begin anew promptly once Agnes was over, and they would continue long after. As early as June 26, advocates for the Salem Church Dam on the Rappahannock noted that it would have prevented the flooding of Fredericksburg, an assertion that opponents claimed was not enough on its own to justify construction.[317] Generally speaking, industry and business representatives favored flood control projects proposed in earlier U.S. Army Corps of Engineers studies, while environmentalists opposed the destruction of existing habitats dams and other projects would cause. Others argued new dams would be inadequate in the event of massive storms like Agnes and would likely encourage floodplain development by fostering a false sense of security. Some even believed the low-interest loans of NFIP were counterproductive insofar as they lessened the cost to the individual or business of choosing to locate in a floodplain. Opponents of floodplain restrictions countered that while parks and other vacant space in floodplains would limit the damage incurred during a disaster, the communities would then forgo substantial tax revenue that could be used to meet other needs.[318]

With recovery now fully underway as communities transitioned from cleanup efforts to securing financial assistance, the process of assessment also advanced. This included not just the compilation of damage estimates but also evaluation of disaster preparation and response. While an official analysis might take some time, the public's assessment of the latter is typically almost immediate and was quite prompt in the case of Agnes. Just as there would inevitably be reflections on community unity and expressions of gratitude to responders and volunteers—and these were numerous and widespread with Agnes—so too would there inevitably be strong critiques.

In hard-hit Prince William County in northern Virginia, a local newspaper, the *Potomac News*, characterized the response of officials, organizations and the county's people as "marvelous." But it also noted duplication, a lack of coordination and, most troublingly, difficulty getting accurate information, citing in particular rumors about dams breaking, roads and bridges failing and the need to boil drinking water.[319] Farmville's *Herald* praised the Farmville National Guard unit, the Coast Guard Auxiliary, the Civil Air Patrol, U.S. Army Reservists, state and federal evaluation teams and utility company workers. It also lauded the "cooperation of county personnel and equipment, the work of police and firemen, and the whole army of private and official aid coming in from adjoining areas," which it asserted "added up to a story of success, endurance, perseverance, determination and human kindness which will be remembered long after Agnes' fury is gone." But in the same article, the *Herald* noted the need for quick means of communication to state and federal relief agencies, earlier control of sightseers and more rapid availability of emergency supplies and equipment.[320]

The *Richmond Times Dispatch* described the disaster response machinery of Agnes as "well-oiled" and remarked that it "got off to a quick start to meet the initial emergency" but characterized the process as "sputtering a week later when it came to the tedium of providing long-term relief." Governor Holton, according to the newspaper, had nothing but praise for the federal assistance, but the newspaper reported that confusion increased when representatives of the president's Office of Emergency Preparedness arrived and began issuing conflicting statements about when flood relief would be available. In fact, when the first disaster assistance office opened in Richmond, only one federal representative was there.[321]

Criticism of local efforts was most pronounced in the city of Richmond. Less than a week after the floodwaters receded, the president of the Farmers' Markets Merchants Association announced he would sue the city for the damages he had incurred as a result of the flooding, noting that unlike in the case of Camille he thought this time the merchants could win. Another officer of the association questioned why yet again, as in Camille, the pumping station could not operate during the flood, exclaiming that the merchants of the association were apparently "'the whipping boys' for the city."[322]

Emotions were also raw in the Fulton Bottom part of the city. "They made all kinds of provisions downtown," one resident remarked to a reporter on June 25. "They don't give a dam [*sic*] about us." After the damage from Camille, he explained, he expected someone would do something about Giles Creek, the immediate source of the periodic flooding, but that had not occurred, and he thought he knew why—repeated flooding would drive property values down so that RRHA could buy the area up more cheaply.[323] By June 29, Agnes had forced forty-nine families out of the Fulton area. Since the Red Cross had already closed its East End Middle School shelter, officials scrambled to find other locations, at first putting men up in YMCA rooms and putting families in efficiency apartments funded by the Red Cross.[324]

By Friday, June 30, frustration resulted in about one hundred Fulton residents, led by Reverend W.F. Richardson, the chair of the Fulton Advisory Council, to pile into two church buses and take a ride to the offices of the RRHA, where they presented a list of demands. Among them the residents asked that temporary housing be provided for all displaced Fulton residents, that the RRHA "immediately" begin residential construction in Fulton to demonstrate its commitment to the goals of the Fulton renewal plan and that all the provisions of the original renewal plan—particularly that no resident be relocated outside Fulton against their wishes—be kept. The RRHA chief executive demurred and then departed allegedly for another meeting. On his departure, the residents began what was effectively a sit-in, aware that they would likely be arrested if they did not depart the building by the end of the day. A little before 6:00 p.m. the situation was resolved when RRHA authorities announced that several houses deemed suitable would be available for people to move into that night, and on the following day a disaster center would open at a nearby school.[325]

The respite was temporary, however. A week later, the executive of the RRHA found himself back with Reverend Richardson in front of about 125 people at Rising Mount Zion Baptist Church, where the crowd wanted him to respond to a list of eight demands Fulton residents had put forward. Before he spoke, the crowd listened to what a reporter described as a "fiery" speech from state senator (and future Virginia governor) L. Douglas Wilder. After about ninety minutes the meeting broke up when Reverend Richardson announced the Fulton community would have to take their case to Washington—urban renewal, he claimed, was destroying Fulton.[326]

When he visited the state on June 28, Vice President Spiro T. Agnew lauded Virginia's civil defense program as one of the best.[327] Approximately two and a half months later, on September 15, the state's office of civil defense issued its own report on Hurricane Agnes. It included a brief evaluation of the office's performance and recommendations for improvement.

Among the strengths of the recent effort, the report commented favorably on the leadership, attitude and responsiveness of action officers, a number of whom brought with them experience from Camille. The report's authors also expressed their view that the Commonwealth of Virginia Natural Disaster Assistance Relief Plan (COVANDAP) proved a reasonable tool for operating during a disaster, recognizing that some of the limitations experienced were associated with local civil defense personnel having only had the plan for a short time before Agnes arrived. Last, officials considered it advantageous that various organizations were physically represented at the emergency operations center, noting that contact and coordination with those organizations during the event was far easier than with those who did not have resident representatives.[328]

During the disaster, Governor Holton expressed his belief that the civil defense plan was working "excellently," and that despite the tragedy of fatalities and property damage, no lives appeared to have been lost as a result of a failure to evacuate.[329] While civil defense officials overall were also pleased with the execution of the plan, they did recommend a variety of changes, some infrastructure-based and others operational. Most important among the former, officials at headquarters found the emergency operations facilities to be "very inadequate." There simply was not enough space for everyone, nor was there sufficient telephone and radio communications equipment. Both of these shortcomings apparently did not exist in the facility used the prior December when testing the plan during Exercise "Katy." In terms of operations, many staff believed some form of internal operations plan was needed that described specific assignments for specific personnel. They proposed, for example that perhaps all regional coordinators, who presumably knew their localities and local officials best, should serve as action officers at the state's emergency operations center, while assistant regional coordinators operated in the field and addressed special localized problems. Additionally, they suggested clarifying the roles of administrative staff and the forms they used during operations. Too many messages during Agnes did not adequately identify the caller, their location or their authority. Finally, as mentioned earlier, staff recommended modifications to the damage assessment approach. Both unfamiliarity with state plans at the local level and duplication at the state level caused problems in damage assessment. Report authors recommended a central clearinghouse for the receipt and tabulation of damage information, as well as increased stress on the need for accurate assessments in order to determine the scope and severity of a problem and to establish the requisite boundaries for a disaster declaration.[330]

Although the office of civil defense evaluation also described as excellent overall federal coordination and assistance "on all levels," some of the strongest criticism concerned this coordination. On the whole, state civil defense staff felt the National Weather Service, in collaboration with the state police and the office of civil defense, provided acceptable, but not excellent, advance notice of potential flood emergencies. Everyone would benefit, they suggested, from some sort of statewide system not reliant on telephone communication networks. During a disaster, the latter might be out of service due to downed lines or be understaffed.[331] The National Oceanic and Atmospheric Administration (NOAA) report, issued in February 1973, largely supported this finding, concluding that "flash flood warnings and forecasts of river crests were timely and allowed effective action" and that the "response of local actions groups was positive," but communication of information to the public was sometimes "inadequate, because of the time-consuming nature of telephone dissemination."[332]

Most discouraging, however, for state civil defense staff appeared to be ignorance on the part of federal coordinating offices of how the disaster assistance program in the state was supposed to work, which led to numerous misunderstandings between state and federal officials. The state's disaster assistance plan, for example, outlined clear areas of authority and responsibility with regard to disaster assistance centers—the state coordinating officer was responsible for site selection, administration and operations. According to the evaluators, the center in Lynchburg was the most successful in the state—and the only one operated by the state. All the others were federal centers, and according to the evaluators, the only one that "provided even close to adequate service was in Covington."[333]

In the September report, thirteen individual state agencies and four quasi-public and private organizations also provided their own chronologies and evaluations of performance, and they also were not uniformly positive. Beyond, as mentioned earlier, recommending the use of state police and local reports for initial damage estimates, the state's director of engineering and buildings echoed concerns about a lack of clarity regarding state and federal responsibilities in practice. He also emphasized the need for both a clear statement of the role of local and regional civil defense coordinators and for lists of official contacts at the local level with whom state and federal officials should be in contact (e.g., city managers).[334] The Department of Military Affairs (Virginia National

Guard) report also cited a number of deficiencies, among them incomplete intelligence from both civil defense and guard personnel; insufficient civil defense training at the county, city and local levels; in-house guard confusion about logistics authority and responsibility; and the need for a logistics and administration communication network separate from the mission communication network. They also asserted that when active-duty army units arrived, they were not properly equipped with adequate sleeping equipment and had failed to make advance housing and food supply arrangements, which placed an unanticipated burden on Virginia Army National Guard personnel. Additionally, by placing an army liaison officer in the city of Richmond's emergency operations center, the army disrupted the assistance request process that was supposed to flow to the state's civil defense office and from there to the National Guard or active duty forces.[335]

In subsequent presentations before the public, civil defense officials remarked that although the natural disaster assistance relief plan was a vast improvement over what had existed during Camille, and was of real value during Agnes, "no localities are adequately prepared." Two-thirds of the 134 jurisdictions in the state at the time had either unpaid volunteer coordinators or existing employees holding the post without additional compensation.[336]

Assessing the cost of Agnes in fatalities and property damage is sobering. By July 20, the state determined there were twelve fatalities, one person missing and thirty-two people injured.[337] The true death toll was at least fifteen and most likely as high as seventeen (see Appendix II). As tragic as these deaths are, they were far fewer than had occurred during Camille, where fatalities exceeded one hundred people. Officials repeatedly stressed, most notably in Nelson County, that both advance warning and memories of Camille played a critical role in reducing the death toll. A Nelson County rescue squad spokesperson remarked during Agnes that lives were saved not only because of the advance warning but also because people "remember the last time and they don't want to get caught."[338]

While its death toll was far less than that of Camille, Agnes outstripped the former in damage. The storm destroyed or damaged more than 600 miles of roads and 103 bridges. It also destroyed more than 200 residences and damaged another 6,000; 50 businesses were wiped out and more than 500 damaged. Almost 1,200 motor vehicles were lost. Utilities in the state experienced more than $54 million in damages among communications, electricity, gas, water, sewage and railroad infrastructure. Other public facilities, including parks and 114 school buildings (71 in Fairfax County), witnessed damage amounting to more than $2.5 million, while Agnes also wreaked havoc among streams, dikes, levees and waterway channels.[339] More than 7 million pounds of food had to be destroyed as a result of flood damage, and the USDA distributed more than 11,000 pounds of food to approximately 5,500 people.[340] Finally, Agnes caused more than $14 million in damage to the state's agricultural sector. Its floodwaters denuded the topsoil and destroyed or damaged fencing as well as farm ponds, streams and equipment. Agnes left more than 30,000 acres of farmland unproductive, wiped out more than 10,000 head of livestock and destroyed more than 175,000 acres of crops, particularly corn and grains like barley and oats that were near harvest.[341]

Other damages would take some time to manifest themselves. One of these would be attributable to the destruction caused by massive amounts of fresh water flowing down Virginia rivers into marine estuaries. On June 23, the state health department prohibited the harvesting of oysters and clams for direct market consumption because of potential contaminants in the floodwaters. Experts later characterized the threat to oyster bays as "extremely serious," for when hit by fresh water, oysters close and can last only about a week in that condition before dying. A die-off of the oyster population would be a serious blow to a Virginia oyster industry already struggling with more strict shellfish sanitation rules.[342] In fact, the threat to the shellfish industry as a result of Agnes led at the end of July to limited disaster declarations for twenty Virginia counties and nine cities, among them coastal plain counties that were otherwise unaffected by Agnes, like Accomack, Isle of Wight, Lancaster, Matthews, Middlesex, Northampton, Northumberland, Surry, Westmoreland and York. Not until July 20 did Virginia begin lifting the first bans on shellfish harvesting, and it was not until October 5 that it lifted all restrictions.[343]

Other long-term damage estimates for lost tourism, commercial and sport fishing; small boat damage; and channel dredging would come in subsequent years. By the middle of September 1972, however, all told the official office of civil defense estimate placed the cost of the damage from Agnes in Virginia at $165,772,400, or the equivalent of more than $1.2 billion in 2023 dollars. This figure would increase to over $200 million (almost $1.5 billion in 2023 dollars) over time as damage and cost estimates became more accurate and comprehensive. But while it is unlikely that the actual cost of such a disaster can ever truly be measured to everyone's satisfaction, one thing is certain: Agnes was devastating for many of those individuals and communities who experienced it.

5

AFTERMATH

A gnes of course did not stop at Virginia. Refreshed off the coast of Norfolk on June 22, Agnes made landfall once again on Long Island. Absorbed into the circulation of a dominant secondary low from the Ohio Valley, Agnes looped inland along the New York and Pennsylvania border, dropping massive amounts of rain on the river basins of the Susquehanna, Schuylkill and Alleghany in Pennsylvania and the Genesee and Chemung in New York. Pennsylvania suffered the worst. There, Agnes caused almost fifty deaths and damaged or destroyed ten and twenty times, respectively, the number of homes it had in Virginia. Conditions were particularly dangerous for a time in Wilkes-Barre, Pennsylvania, where hundreds of people found themselves trapped in their homes by floodwaters.[344] By June 25, Agnes was moving into Canada.

Federal relief efforts soon became enveloped in the politics of the upcoming 1972 presidential election. Richard Nixon had been president when Camille struck in 1969, and it was his head of the Office of Emergency Preparedness, retired brigadier general, West Point graduate and Rhodes Scholar George Lincoln, who, after experiencing the shortcomings of federal and state coordination during Camille, implemented the idea of "one-stop" disaster assistance centers. But when Congress pursued post-Camille rebuilding funding that contained both an organizational restructuring and an end to discrimination in disaster assistance, the Nixon administration pushed back against what it already believed to be generous assistance terms. The compromise that emerged was the Disaster Relief Act of 1970.[345]

Top: Floodwaters in Wilkes Barre, Pennsylvania. *Courtesy NOAA/NSW.*

Bottom: President Nixon meets flood victims in Pennsylvania. *Courtesy Richard Nixon Presidential Library and Museum.*

Agnes now presented Nixon with an opportunity under the Disaster Relief Act to win support ahead of the November presidential elections, particularly in Pennsylvania, which he had lost in 1968 to Hubert Humphrey. Nixon made a brief two-hour tour of Harrisburg on June 24 and then sent Vice President Agnew to visit the affected states on June 28. Flood victims in Pennsylvania were exasperated by the situation in the state and unsatisfied with the federal response. And in their Democratic governor Milton Shapp, they had both a boisterous advocate and a harsh critic of the president. It was Shapp who called the meeting of mid-Atlantic governors in Harrisburg on June 25 that Virginia governor Linwood Holton attended. In the background, of course, was the suspicion created on June 17, just a few days before Agnes arrived, when five men were caught breaking into Democratic National Committee headquarters in Washington, D.C.'s Watergate hotel.

In the ensuing weeks, the Nixon administration sparred with those who argued for more generous assistance terms, in particular those who wished to provide grants instead of loans to flood victims. Nixon proffered instead a mix, accompanied by the prospect of a low interest rate of 1 percent and forgiveness of the first $5,000 of any loan. He reportedly asserted that this was "a sure thing in Pennsylvania."[346] Accounts attribute numerous individuals with declaring Agnes the worst natural disaster in American history. When Nixon began the process of selling his plan to the public and Congress, he used similar language, starting with a brief radio address on July 12 in which he characterized Agnes as the "worst natural disaster in the whole of American history."[347] Announcing his intention to recommend a record level of disaster recovery relief, he followed the radio address with a formal proposal to Congress on July 17. Dubbed the Agnes Recovery Act of 1972, Nixon proposed not only the loan forgiveness and low interest provisions but also a supplemental appropriation of more than $1.5 billion.[348]

The legislation proved controversial, as to some it smacked of political opportunism and electoral politics, particularly insofar as it included disaster relief provisions that the Nixon administration had rejected in other bills, including in the fight over the Disaster Relief Act of 1970.[349] Such sudden generosity led some to question why this largess had not been extended to Rapid City, South Dakota, an area victimized by flooding a few weeks before Agnes. When Nixon responded to the criticism by adding South Dakota the very next day, it led to requests by democratic California congressman Alan Cranston for retroactive relief for the San Fernando earthquake of 1971 and by Republican senator Ted Stevens of Alaska for an earthquake in 1964. Ultimately, the bill, which Nixon signed on August 20, 1972, made relief retroactive to January 1, 1972, including Agnes and the South Dakota disasters but excluding the others.[350]

For people in Pennsylvania in particular, however, assistance was not coming fast enough. This led to a very angry and public confrontation between citizens of the state and HUD secretary George Romney when the latter visited Pennsylvania on August 9.[351] With the Agnes Recovery Act of 1972 not yet in place, Romney and other federal officials were operating under the Disaster Relief Act of 1970 and under the direction of the president's Office of Emergency Preparedness. Predictably, some of the shortcomings—inexperienced personnel (many of them new, temporary employees in some areas), confusion about authority and responsibility and the paperwork required—which were mentioned in Virginia's after-action analysis, became magnified exponentially in Pennsylvania, where the extent of the damage was so much greater. Particularly problematic was the requirement that the state and individual localities first pay for infrastructure rehabilitation and seek government reimbursement later.[352] George Romney proved a convenient scapegoat for all of these problems, and on August 12, Nixon appointed Scranton, Pennsylvania native and deputy director of the president's Office of Management and Budget (OMB), Frank Carlucci, head of the Agnes relief effort. Carlucci relocated to Wilkes-Barre and chose to live in a trailer, largely winning over the people of the area. After securing reelection to the presidency in overwhelming fashion (including winning Pennsylvania) in November 1972, however, Nixon ordered the recall of Carlucci (who left in December), moved to restrict Agnes benefits, canceled the Farm and Home Administration (FHA) program for victims, resisted attempts to expand the time limit for loan applications and vetoed attempts to apply the terms of Agnes recovery legislation to other disasters.[353]

While the Agnes Recovery Act of 1972 addressed financial assistance for the victims of Agnes, other legislation eventually took shape to change disaster management operations. In Virginia, the general assembly adopted the Commonwealth of Virginia Emergency Services and Disaster Law of 1973. This statute created a state Office of Emergency Services, which was ultimately renamed the Virginia Department of Emergency Management (VDEM) in 2000. Administratively under the secretary of transportation and public safety under normal conditions, the office reverts to the operational control of the governor in the event of a declared disaster. The law made clear once again that political subdivisions bore responsibility for local disaster preparedness and coordination of response and required that they have a director of emergency services, authorizing them to set up an office for such services if they wished.[354]

At the federal level, Agnes ultimately inspired a number of operational changes. Among them, the subsequent Disaster Relief Act of 1974 forced on localities the obligation to prepare for disasters and to take steps in advance to mitigate their effects. After Agnes, Nixon had moved disaster preparedness out of the Office of the President and into the Department of Housing and Urban Development. Now, under the new disaster relief act, the responsibility was moved again, but this time to a new Federal Disaster Assistance Administration (FDAA), which also could provide grants to states for disaster warning systems and planning. The act also required that relevant federal agencies be prepared to issue warnings at the state and local level. This requirement was directed largely at the National Weather Service. After-action reports generally lauded the performance of the Weather Service during Agnes, but there were significant deficiencies caused by the failure of localities to subscribe to the paid national warning system (NAWAS) operated by the National Oceanic and Atmospheric Administration. Eventually, additional funding resulted in the system broadcasting round-the-clock every day. Also, but unrelated to the act, Nixon renamed the federal civil defense apparatus the Defense Civil Preparedness Agency (DCPA) and moved it out from under the Department of the Army and into the Department of Defense. At least one scholar has characterized the Disaster Relief Act of 1974 as a "change in the course of U.S. disaster policy," insofar as it both mandated disaster preparation by localities in order to qualify for subsequent disaster benefits and also provided funds for such planning. By doing so it served as a catalyst for professionalizing the emergency management of disasters. Later, in 1978, President Jimmy Carter, after discussions with Frank Carlucci, consolidated most federal disaster response activities into the Federal Emergency Management Administration (FEMA).[355]

Debates over floodplain regulations and the role of a national flood insurance program continued. As they had in the past, some argued for restrictions on floodplain development while others asserted the adverse commercial impact of such restrictions made flood control projects like dams, levees and dikes more appropriate. The Nixon administration aspired to shift the cost of managing floods back to the states and away from flood control projects and so wanted disaster relief tied to state plans and measures to reduce risk. He tried to accomplish this with the Flood Disaster Protection Act of 1973, which in its original form would have required that localities enroll in the National Flood Insurance Program and thus also enact the necessary ordinances addressing development in floodplains. One goal was to prevent the practice of allowing people to rebuild in a floodplain after a disaster. Public opposition, however, scuttled the relevant requirements with the result that the law, by providing the heavily subsidized insurance without meaningful restrictions, actually encouraged more residential use of flood-prone areas. Eventually, insurance companies stopped writing the subsidized insurance until by 1983 the federal government had to run the entire program, with the majority of claims coming from repetitive floods of the same properties.[356] There have been repeated attempts to reform the system over time, with limited success.

In the ensuing years after Agnes, reports from a variety of sources continued to assess the impact of the storm. Several of them relevant to Virginia detailed the effects of Agnes on the country's largest estuary, the Chesapeake Bay, beginning with a report prepared for the U.S. Army Corps of Engineers' Philadelphia District by the Chesapeake Bay Research Council in January 1973, followed by others, including a report for the Baltimore District in March 1975. The latter addressed subjects such as shore erosion, sedimentation, salinity and effects on bay marine life. Abnormal shore erosion from Agnes was limited given the storm's light winds. Additionally, with relatively light sediment loads in tributaries on the west side of the bay and only modest rainfall on the Eastern Shore, there was little sediment carried into the bay from those areas. From the north, however, the Susquehanna River discharged more sediment during Agnes than in the preceding ten years combined. When the normal circulatory patterns of the bay reestablished themselves, however, much of that sediment remained in the bay's northern reaches, with the result that floodwaters deposited only about an additional centimeter as far south as the Rappahannock River. Furthermore, although the floodwaters carried various compounds into the bay, including dissolved nitrogen and phosphorus, as well as trace metals and pesticides, the report's authors concluded that these were insufficient on their own to cause large-scale mortality in bay species.[357]

As anticipated early in the disaster, however, changes in salinity were to have a substantial impact. According to the corps report, species like finfish, blue crabs and hard-shell clams experienced only minor and temporary difficulties. Finfish simply moved downstream to areas of appropriate salinity, while blue crabs were only temporarily displaced; hard clam losses were minor and limited primarily to the York River. Soft-shell clams and oysters were the two species that experienced the greatest mortality due to Agnes. The former were not a major commercial activity in Virginia, but in Maryland, where they were, over 90 percent were destroyed by higher salinity and water temperature. Reproduction of survivors was high in 1972, but contamination (not necessarily definitively tied to Agnes) forced closure of the harvest in 1972.[358]

For Virginia, the most significant impact was on the oyster population, particularly on the public oyster bars of the Potomac's tributaries. More than half of the mature oysters there died, while only 5 percent died on those of the James, York and Rappahannock Rivers. Most troubling, however, was that although the oyster harvest of 1972–73 was excellent, reproduction was very low. This combination of high harvest and low reproduction augured a long recovery period. The only silver lining for the oyster population of the bay was that Agnes had also destroyed much of the oyster drills population. A type of predatory sea snail that attacks oysters, they are slow to repopulate an area and thus would not contribute to retarding the recovery of bay oysters.[359]

Virginia responded well in the aftermath to the damage Agnes caused to roads and bridges. While estimates of the cost escalated, within a few

Cleanup and repair near bridge at Wingina. *Courtesy Library of Virginia.*

Bridge repair near Shawsville in Montgomery County. *Courtesy Library of Virginia.*

weeks, highway travel was back to normal, and of 103 bridges destroyed or damaged, only 24 remained closed. In fact, later in the year officials lamented that their efficiency had worked to their disadvantage when Congress adjourned without approving a new bill for highway aid—unlike other states, Virginia had already spent most of its funds.[360]

For the widespread Virginia communities affected by Agnes, the storm's aftermath took many forms. Unfortunately, soon after the flooding everyone had to be wary of potential scams. On July 25, for example, the *Roanoke Times* advised people to be on the alert when buying used automobiles, as some people were selling flood-impaired vehicles without disclosing damage.[361] In August, the Prince William County Board of Supervisors had to respond to rumors of contractors inflating estimates and charging flood victims for unnecessary items and services. It adopted a sixty-day ordinance that required all home improvement contractors to be licensed and bonded in the county.[362]

Local officials also in the immediate aftermath of Agnes had to deal with complaints that seemed to pale given the magnitude of the challenges ahead.

One concerned mosquitoes. Just a few days after Agnes, a self-described Pentagon employee living at Broad Run in Loudoun County complained to the secretary of health, education and welfare about mosquitoes, claiming that the local health department was doing nothing about the problem. The state health department called the county health department and learned that it was, in fact, spraying the area with a strong product that could be used safely only every few days. At approximately the same time, Rockbridge County called the state office of civil defense regarding mosquitoes, saying the health department did not know how to handle their "BIG" (emphasis in the original) problem. When asked, local health officials explained that this had been a months-long problem, exacerbated by Agnes, that involved several square miles of private land that they could not legally access, much less identify resources to handle.[363] Later, in August, a delegation of residents appeared before the Augusta Board of County Supervisors asking for relief from a mosquito problem that had gotten so bad in some areas in the eastern side of the county that people were unable to go outside "to mow their lawns or work in gardens." Augusta's county executive agreed to look into an experimental spraying program, but a little more than a week later the mosquito problem subsided, and officials deemed spraying unjustified.[364]

For some areas, the aftermath of Agnes occasionally provided pleasant distractions to go along with the sometimes overwhelming and discouraging task of recovery. Near Bremo Bluff, for example, the floodwaters of Agnes both destroyed the railroad bridge across the James River and uncovered a cache of Confederate-made Minié balls from the Civil War. The latter led some locals on a fascinating search for their origin.[365] Most of the time, however, the aftermath of Agnes was serious and sobering, sometimes leading to needed change and other times to change some would lament.

In the city of Alexandria in northern Virginia, Congress pursued additional funding for what was known as the Four Mile Run East and West Levee System. Reauthorized in 1974, completed by 1984 and periodically dredged and repaired, the flood-control channel has effectively eliminated the periodic flooding that used to plague the area.

South of the city, in Prince William County, the residents of the town of Occoquan still did not like the idea of a new bridge going up at the eastern end of town, but with Agnes's destruction of their historic bridge, the fight had largely gone out of them on the issue. Almost a month after the flood, divers from Fort Belvoir's Seventy-Seventh Engineering Company spent a couple of hours in the river looking for the wreckage of the old bridge to ensure it did not hamper navigation. They also searched for a plaque the town's historical society had placed on the bridge. All they found were some girders.[366] The town mayor expressed concern that town businesses, some of which had applied for federal assistance, might fail or leave if a replacement bridge did not go up soon. By the middle of August, state officials had responded by putting up a temporary H-10 army bridge at the site of the old bridge until a new one could be constructed at the town's eastern edge. Later, the state, with the support of the town, constructed a bicycle and pedestrian bridge where the old bridge had once stood.[367]

The Route 123 crossing of the Occoquan River turned out not to be the only bridge problem in the immediate area. Unexpectedly, on July 19 Agnes struck a late blow and added to her bridge tally when the northbound span of the U.S. Route 1 bridge just to the east of the town collapsed into the Occoquan River due to damage from the storm. While inspections took place, both spans of the bridge had to be closed, creating what was described at the time as the worst traffic jam in the area's history.[368]

A year later in the town of Occoquan, most of the businesses that received federal assistance after Agnes were operating at pre-flood levels. One

Collapse of US Route 1 Bridge in Prince William County. *Courtesy Library of Virginia.*

exception was Colonial Funeral Home, out of which some thirty caskets had allegedly escaped during Agnes, floating into the river and through the streets of town. The funeral home had not yet tried to reopen; all that had survived Agnes was a hearse driven to higher ground. With the new bridge at the eastern end of town only half finished, the temporary army bridge continued to bring Route 123 traffic through Occoquan. While that sufficed, the stream that flowed through and underneath the town was still a problem. Agnes had filled with concrete and steel the conduit constructed by the Civil Works Administration in 1933, and a few years after Agnes things worsened when the remnants of Hurricane Eloise came through the area in September 1975, once again generating flash flooding from a local stream and causing the Occoquan River to overflow its banks.[369] Although the county provided most of the funding to repair the drainage system, the town struggled to find the remainder. To make matters worse, experiencing yet another flash flood from the same stream frustrated many town residents, who attributed the recurring problem to what they considered to be inadequately planned development in the local Lake Ridge community on the heights to the west of town. As a result, over the next few years, the goodwill engendered when volunteers from that community had helped clean up the town after Agnes diminished, with one town resident who appeared before the county board of supervisors referring to the neighboring community as "Flood Ridge."[370]

In the rest of Prince William County a year after Agnes, many were still working to remedy the storm's effects, though progress had been made. Where residential damage had been heaviest in the west, Bull Run and other streams remained choked with debris and periodically flooded during heavy rains, but funding was available to begin a remediation project that summer. Dumfries, in the southeastern part of the county, planned to clean and straighten Quantico Creek. Near Manassas, officials removed a small bridge in Ben Lomond Park that residents of the flooded Sudley subdivision claimed obstructed water and contributed to Agnes's flooding. Perhaps most importantly, however, the board of county supervisors had adopted the requisite regulations to qualify for the National Flood Insurance Program, and some 282 people had secured policies. The town of Occoquan would eventually follow. A few years after Agnes, both Manassas and Manassas Park detached from Prince William County and became independent cities.[371]

As mentioned earlier, on the Rappahannock the flooding of Fredericksburg reignited debate over constructing the Salem Church Dam. Although opposition prevented the dam from ever being built, that did not stop the normally authoritative *Encyclopedia Britannica* from momentarily

Coffins from a funeral home floated into the streets of Occoquan. *Courtesy Occoquan Historical Society.*

creating it in the minds of some when it erroneously described the dam as existing and standing 194 feet high and 8,850 feet long in the 1980s.[372] To the west near Waynesboro and surrounding Augusta County, the sentiment toward dams was more favorable. Little more than a few months after Agnes departed, work began on clearing the channel of the South River, including through the city of Waynesboro, and in 1980 the last of eleven flood-control dams in the South River watershed was built at Jones Hollow, just east of the city.

Among the communities along the James, the aftermath was uneven. During Agnes, some in Scottsville expressed certainty about the town's recovery. Watching the floodwaters rise from inside Scottsville's National Bank and Trust Company, one businessman told a reporter that people would not leave Scottsville. "It's a lot of hard work," he said to the reporter, "and a whole lot of money going down the James. But I think these people with the heart they've got they'll come back. They are not going to leave."[373] A year later, things were not so certain. According to the town's mayor, all sixty-two of the commercial buildings in town were in use before Agnes; a year later the number was down to forty, and two of the largest taxpaying businesses, the IGA food store and Silco department store, had left. Many now had flood insurance but considered the coverage for business contents paltry.[374] In 1985, the U.S. Army Corps of Engineers built a levee around the lowest part of the town, effectively preventing future flooding. Scottsville survived. Meanwhile, Vernard Hurt apparently continued to reside in nearby Howardsville, despite the tragedy he had experienced there in 1969 with Camille and in 1972 with Agnes. Records show that he passed away there in September 1977 at age fifty-five.[375]

At Cartersville, some feared Agnes's destruction of the old wood and iron bridge across the James would be the death knell of the community. Although the state promised a replacement bridge, residents and businesses feared that by the time it was operational it would be too late; customers and vendors would be used to doing business elsewhere. With the state ruling out a temporary bridge as impractical, a general store owner and his son created a makeshift ferry out of a small motor-powered barge on pontoons. Users of the ferry had to park their cars and walk up a wooden plank to board and, on reaching the other side, had to walk up the bluff or take a pickup truck shuttle service the ferry operators offered. The state responded to the pleas of the community soon after and announced it would institute a temporary ferry service until the new bridge was in place. After the new bridge was constructed, the state turned ownership of the old bridge's remaining end spans and stone piers over to the Cartersville Bridge Association for preservation.[376]

Columbia was ultimately not as fortunate as Scottsville or Cartersville. The community's population allegedly peaked in 1870 at 311 people, but with major floods in 1870 and 1877, more between 1900 and 1910, yet another in 1954 and then Camille and Agnes in rapid succession, the writing seemed to be on the wall. Another major storm caused near-Agnes flood levels in 1985. Over the succeeding decades people abandoned the town, leaving empty buildings. By 2015, the community had some thirty-six registered voters who approved a referendum to

Locals view washed out Route 45 bridge over the James River at Cartersville. *Courtesy Library of Virginia.*

disincorporate. After the state accordingly revoked its charter, Columbia no longer existed as a town and once again came under the sole authority of Fluvanna County.[377]

Agnes also likely played a role in the ultimate demise of the historic neighborhood of Fulton Bottom in Richmond, as repeated flooding took its toll. Prior to Agnes, federal legislation, specifically the Uniform Relocation Assistance and Real Properties Acquisition Act of 1970, had already made relocating more attractive. Introducing fair compensation for forced displacement, the act removed a problem that had typically plagued urban renewal efforts—with market values depressed in the area allegedly needing renewal, the funds provided to those being displaced were inadequate for securing housing elsewhere. By increasing the compensation, the act made relocation financially feasible, encouraging the departure of those who otherwise might stay. One analysis of the situation in Fulton Bottom notes that when President Nixon announced a moratorium on urban renewal funds in 1973, Fulton residents grew concerned about a potential lost opportunity and demanded that RRHA purchase their properties immediately so that they did not miss out. Within a few years, the community vanished.[378]

The long-term national impact of Agnes was substantial. As we have seen, it reaffirmed the wisdom of moving civil defense planning away from the old focus on enemy attack and toward a focus on natural disasters. While President Nixon's politicization of the Agnes response was not the beginning of using disasters for political advantage, it certainly exacerbated a trend that continues to lead to recriminations today. On the other hand, Nixon's response to Agnes, by insisting on state and local disaster planning and preparation—and by providing funding for such efforts—contributed to the professionalization of emergency management. Agnes also reignited the debate that continues to this day about where on the spectrum society should fall between accommodating nature through land use policies and attempting to control it through public works projects. And by virtue of being one of the first major natural disasters to hit the country after the creation of the National Flood Insurance Program, Agnes started us down a path of constantly reevaluating how best to address the losses of

The flooded IGA Food Mart in Scottsville. *Courtesy Library of Virginia.*

those in a disaster's path and the level of responsibility we should expect them and their community to assume.

Despite its long-term impact, in the short attention span of the popular national consciousness, Agnes soon vanished from prominence. At the beginning it had to compete for space with the Vietnam War, a looming pilots' strike, the presidential election and a wide array of other topics; for a few short days it pushed almost all of them from the headlines. But these others would soon reassert their dominance in the public eye. For many communities throughout the Commonwealth of Virginia, Agnes dominated the mental landscape a little longer. Larger urban and semi-urban areas, no matter the level of damage, survived, generally continued to grow and moved onward. Smaller communities showed the most variation. Some faded away, but of those that survived, few reverted entirely to their pre-Agnes condition. Instead, as Agnes faded into the background, they gradually transformed, like all surviving communities do, in a manner influenced by their history, location and people. Despite the subsequent variation among them, however, the one thing all of these communities, large and small, would retain in common was that they all had experienced Agnes, and of those who remained, none would likely ever forget it.

EPILOGUE

Hurricanes and tropical storms continue to be a regular occurrence for many on the East and Gulf Coasts of the United States, not to mention the Caribbean, Central America and other parts of the world where they go by other names. According to one analysis, since 1980 hurricanes have accounted for some 50 percent of all natural disasters in the United States that exceed $1 billion in damages.[379] And climate scientists regularly warn us that their frequency and intensity are likely to increase, along with those of other weather extremes, as mankind's contributions to global climate change continue. In fact, while writing this volume, Tropical Storm Hilary (previously Hurricane Hilary) became one of the rare such storms to strike California and the southwestern United States, where it generated massive flooding and mudslides.

A year after Agnes, the Saffir-Simpson scale, initially developed in 1971, came into use. Developed by Hebert Saffir and Robert Simpson, who was then the director of the U.S. National Hurricane Center, it divides storms into five categories based on wind speed. As noted in the text, applying the scale retroactively, Agnes barely qualified as a hurricane—and even then, only for a short time—yet the damage she caused was so shocking that officials retired the name in the spring of 1973. As shocking as she was at the time, now, even on an inflation-adjusted basis, Agnes does not make a list of the top ten. Yet she remains nonetheless representative of a preeminent force in nature and a reminder that we show indifference to such power at our peril.

*It serves as scourge to correct the vanity, to humble the pride,
and to chastise the imprudence and arrogance of men.*

—*William Beckford, reacting to the Jamaica hurricane of 1780, from*
A Descriptive Account of the Island of Jamaica, *vol. 1.
(London: T. and J. Egerton, 1790), 90*

VIRGINIA COUNTIES AND CITIES LISTED IN EMERGENCY PROCLAMATION OF JUNE 23, 1972*

COUNTIES

Albemarle	Fauquier	Montgomery
Alleghany	Floyd	Nelson
Amelia	Fluvanna	Nottoway
Amherst	Franklin	Orange
Appomattox	Frederick	Page
Arlington	Giles	Patrick
Augusta	Goochland	Pittsylvania
Bath	Greene	Powhatan
Bedford	Halifax	Prince Edward
Botetourt	Hanover	Prince William
Brunswick	Henrico	Pulaski
Buckingham	Henry	Rappahannock
Campbell	Highland	Richmond
Caroline	King and Queen	Roanoke
Charlotte	King George	Rockbridge
Chesterfield	King William	Rockingham
Clarke	Loudoun	Shenandoah
Culpepper	Louisa	Spotsylvania
Cumberland	Lunenburg	Stafford
Craig	Madison	Warren
Fairfax	Mecklenburg	Westmoreland

CITIES[**]

Alexandria	Lexington
Bedford	Lynchburg
Buena Vista	Martinsville
Charlottesville	Petersburg
Clifton Forge	Radford
Colonial Heights	Richmond
Covington	Roanoke
Danville	Salem
Fairfax	South Boston
Falls Church	Staunton
Fredericksburg	Waynesboro
Harrisonburg	Winchester
Hopewell	

*The original proclamation from President Nixon did not include all the localities identified by Governor Holton but was later amended to do so.

**In Virginia, cities are independent of their surrounding or adjacent counties and therefore are not covered by an emergency declaration for a county but must be identified separately. Towns, however, while having some independent powers, are not independent of the county in which they are located and thus are covered by an emergency declaration for the county of which they are a part.

DEATHS IN VIRGINIA DIRECTLY RELATED TO HURRICANE AGNES

The reported death toll for Hurricane Agnes in Virginia ranges from twelve to seventeen. Virginia's *Report on Tropical Storm Agnes*, dated September 15, 1972, and prepared by the State Office of Civil Defense, reports twelve dead and one missing and may reflect only those *Virginians* who died as a result of Agnes, rather than all those who died *in Virginia* as a result of Agnes.

The highest figure, seventeen, may reflect a combination of the following factors: (1) one or more erroneous press reports that mistake Allen Emanuel Jones and Emanuel Jones as two separate people;* (2) the potential death of two minors whose names were not reported or whose deaths were not subsequently confirmed;** and (3) references to recovered, but at the time unidentified, bodies. The table that follows lists fifteen deaths that the author has confirmed against death certificate records (including one minor) and would appear to document that the death toll is at least fifteen *in* Virginia. If there were, in fact, children traveling with the couple from Illinois, then the death toll *in* Virginia was seventeen. Included in the table is the person's name, age, town/state of residence, occupation, cause of death and approximate location of death. Among the dead were one African American, three veterans of Vietnam and one veteran of World War II.

JUNE 21, 1972

Homer Wilson Comer, sixty-four, Shenandoah, Page County (shop worker, Norfolk & Western Railroad). Found drowned near his home in Shenandoah in Page County.

Donald Douglas Cox, sixty-three, Mt. Vernon, Illinois (minister). Drowned when car was swept off Route 60 near Brick Kiln Branch tributary of the James River in Rockingham County.

Mary Hulen Cox, sixty-one, Mt. Vernon, Illinois (housewife; spouse of Donald Douglas Cox). Drowned when car was swept off Route 60 near Brick Kiln Branch tributary of the James River in Rockingham County.

Francoise M. Craig, thirty-three, Annandale, Fairfax County (housewife). Drowned when swept down Accotink Creek behind 3803 Hillcrest Lane in Fairfax County while firemen were attempting to get her to higher ground.

Frances Sandford Davis, sixty-eight, Centreville, Fairfax County (retired teacher). Drowned when car swept away by floodwaters; found in cow pasture near Pleasant Valley Road in Fairfax County.

Robert Roy Henderson, seventy-nine, Afton, Nelson County (retired cooper, barrel maker). Drowned when car ran into washed out culvert of swollen Taylor Creek in Nelson County and was swept away.

Alfred Henry Johnson, fifty-seven, Centreville, Fairfax County (auto services advisor). Drowned when swept away by floodwaters of Bull Run while in a stalled truck in Fairfax County.

Jerry Donald Romans, twenty-three, rural Virginia (restaurant manager). Drowned when car was surrounded by floodwaters of Marumsco Creek on U.S. Route 1 in Woodbridge, Virginia in Prince William County.

Ovis Willard Whytsell, thirty-nine, Woodbridge, Prince William County (U.S. Army active duty) Flood-related automobile accident at Fort Belvoir, Virginia, in Fairfax County.

Michael Dennis Robey, thirty-four, Great Falls, Fairfax County (retired, U.S. Army). Drowned when car swept off road by floodwaters from Difficult Run in Fairfax County.

JUNE 22, 1972

Timothy W. Arbuckle, fifteen, North Pineallas Park, Florida (student). Died when he fell into a hole and it filled with sand and water, suffocating him near Route 60 and Salisbury Drive in Midlothian, Chesterfield County.

Lorenza(o) Lee Harris, thirty-one, Broad Run, Prince William County (service station worker). Drowned as car was swept away when earthen dam collapsed in the Jackson Hollow Recreational Area by Antioch and Waterfall Roads near Haymarket, Virginia, in Prince William County.

Allen Emanuel Jones, fifty-four, Fairfax County (plumber). Drowned driving across flooded road near 7809 South Lake Drive in the Yorkshire area of Prince William County.

Cecil Corbin O'Bannon, twenty-three, Falls Church (drywall installer). Drowned when boat overturned in floodwaters near Ordway Street and Bull Run in Fairfax County.

UNCONFIRMED POTENTIAL DEATHS

UNCONFIRMED MINORS

Early reports indicated that two children were also in the car with Donald and Mary Cox. Later reports, however, do not mention any children. Whether or not this was because earlier reports were mistaken or because of a subsequent decision not to report on the deaths of minors is unknown. The author could not find any other records suggesting there were children in the vehicle.**

UNCONFIRMED UNIDENTIFIED

Some sources include a reference to an unidentified thirty-three-year-old female who allegedly drowned in an undisclosed locality in Fairfax County.

Some sources include a reference to an alleged drowning in the Arlandria section of Alexandria.

*See, e.g., Lawrence Brown, "Camille Outdone in Destruction: The State," *Richmond Times Dispatch*, June 24, 1972. In this newspaper article's list of the dead, there are entries for both Allen E. Jones of Lorton and Emanuel Jones of Yorkshire. This is one individual, Allen Emanuel Jones of Lorton, Virginia, who died when his car was swept away by floodwaters in the Yorkshire area.

**See, e.g., Stephen Fleming, "Cresting Due Here at 9:00 a.m. at Locks, *Richmond Times Dispatch*, June 23, 1972.

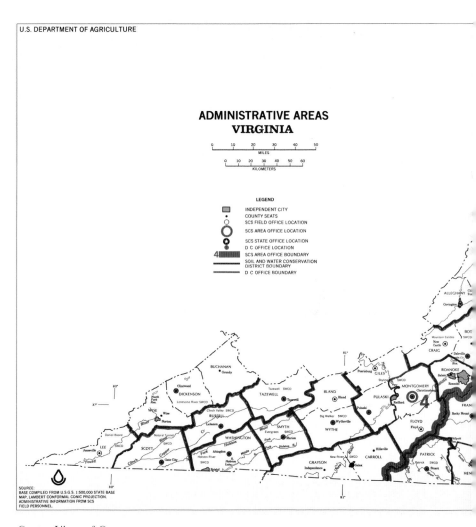

ADMINISTRATIVE AREAS
VIRGINIA

0   10   20   30   40   50
MILES

0   10   20   30   40   50   60
KILOMETERS

LEGEND

☐ INDEPENDENT CITY
· COUNTY SEATS
○ SCS FIELD OFFICE LOCATION
◎ SCS AREA OFFICE LOCATION
✪ SCS STATE OFFICE LOCATION
   D C OFFICE LOCATION
4▦▦▦▦ SCS AREA OFFICE BOUNDARY
   SOIL AND WATER CONSERVATION
   DISTRICT BOUNDARY
   D C OFFICE BOUNDARY

SOURCE:
BASE COMPILED FROM U.S.G.S. 1:500,000 STATE BASE
MAP, LAMBERT CONFORMAL CONIC PROJECTION.
ADMINISTRATIVE INFORMATION FROM SCS
FIELD PERSONNEL.

Courtesy Library of Congress.

APPENDIX III

MAP OF ADMINISTRATIVE AREAS
(INCLUDING COUNTIES) OF VIRGINIA

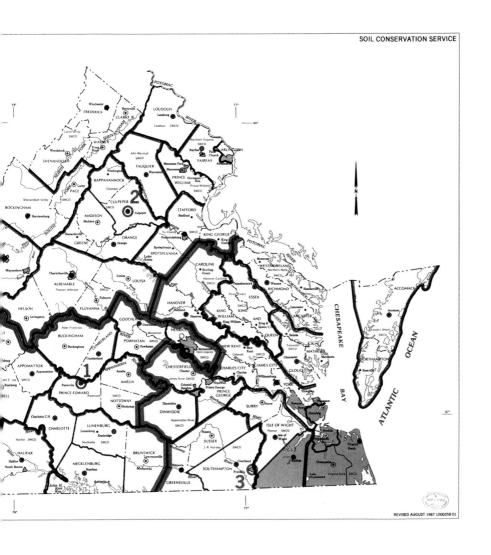

REVISED AUGUST 1987 1000358-01

NOTES

EPIGRAPH

1. As quoted in Beverly Orndorff, "Flood Termed Most Extensive in U.S. History," *Richmond Times-Dispatch*, June 24, 1972.

INTRODUCTION

2. "Possible Hurricane Building," *Playground Daily News* (Fort Walton Beach, FL), June 16, 1972. Susan Eliff set the rocking chair record while participating in Jackson, Tennessee's Sesquicentennial Rocking Chair Marathon, part of the celebration for the 150th anniversary of Jackson's founding. The more than 120 contestants were permitted to take seven-minute breaks periodically, with a first prize of $400 (almost $2,700 today) going to the winner. "Rocking Chair Marathon Set June 20," *Jackson Sun*, June 2, 1972; "121 Contestants in Rocking Chair Marathon," *Jackson Sun*, June 9, 1972.
3. *Pensacola News*, June 16, 1972; "Red Cross Urges Hurricane Safety," *Panama City News-Herald*, June 16, 1972, *Weekender*; Dick Holland, "Storm No. 1 is Born," *Miami News*, June 16, 1972; Kevin Molloy, "Disturbance Near Yucatan Develops into Depression," *Miami Herald*, June 16, 1972; "'Agnes' Blows into a Storm in Caribbean," *Naples Daily News*, June 16, 1972; "Agnes Is Born Off Mexico," *Fort Lauderdale News*, June 16, 1972; "Season's 1st Storm Intensifies," *Boca Raton News*, June 16, 1972; "First

Depression Is Strengthening Off Yucatan Coast," *Tampa Bay Times*, June 16, 1972.

4. "Storm Agnes Builds Punch," *Boston Evening Globe*, June 16, 1972; "Tropical Storm Off Yucatan First of Hurricane Season," *New York Times*, June 17, 1972; "First Hurricane," *Washington Post*, June 18, 1972; *Danville Bee*, June 16, 1972; "Tropical Storm Grows," *Orlando Evening Star*, June 16, 1972.

5. R.H. Simpson and Paul J. Herbert, *Atlantic Hurricane Season of 1972* (Miami, FL: National Hurricane Center, National Weather Service, NOAA, 1973), 323. Sources disagree on the exact number of deaths caused by Agnes, but most appear to agree the number is above 120 and less than 130 (although Simpson and Herbert report "less than 120 lives were lost").

6. The Saffir-Simpson Hurricane Wind Scale was developed in 1971 but was not in use at the time of Agnes. Named after wind engineer Herb Saffir and meteorologist Bob Simpson, it characterizes hurricanes on a scale from 1 to 5 based on wind speed as follows: Category 1 (74 to 95 miles per hour [mph]), Category 2 (96 to 110 mph), Category 3 (111 to 129 mph), Category 4 (130 to 156 mph) and Category 5 (157 and higher mph).

7. Simpson and Herbert, *Atlantic Hurricane Season of 1972*, 325–29.

8. Timothy Kneeland, *Playing Politics with Natural Disaster: Hurricane Agnes, the 1972 Election, and the Origins of FEMA* (Ithaca, NY: Cornell University Press, 2020), 35.

9. Simpson and Herbert, *Atlantic Hurricane Season of 1972*, 329. It appears that a variety of people at the time, almost certainly to some degree echoing the sentiments of their contemporaries, characterized Agnes in this way. In addition to meteorologists Robert Simpson and Paul Herbert, for example, on June 24, 1972, Lieutenant General Frederick Clarke, chief of engineers of the U.S. Army Corps of Engineers, characterized Agnes as "the worst natural disaster in the history of the country." U.S. Army Corps of Engineers, "Hurricane Agnes: Fifty Years Later," July 2022, www.usace.army.mil.

10. U.S. Army Corps of Engineers, "Hurricane Agnes: Fifty Years Later."

1. THE HISTORY AND SCIENCE OF HURRICANES

11. Among the Maya, the god of storms was Hunraken, while among the Arawak-speaking groups of the Caribbean like the Taino it was *hurakán* or *juracán*. *Furacane, haurachana* and *uracan* are all earlier versions of what became the Spanish *huracán* and Portuguese *furacão*. By 1688, the word *hurricane* had been established in English. Robert K. Barnhardt, ed., *The*

Barnhardt Concise Dictionary of Etymology (New York: HarperCollins, 1995); Eric Jay Donlin, *A Furious Sky: The Five-Hundred-Year History of America's Hurricanes* (New York: Liveright Publishing Corporation, 2020), xxv.

12. Samuel Eliot Morison, *Admiral of the Ocean Sea: A Life of Christopher Columbus* (Boston: Little, Brown and Company, 1970), 589–90 (Morison believes that storms Columbus encountered in 1494 and 1495 were also hurricanes); Donlin, *Furious Sky*, 4–6.

13. Donlin, *Furious Sky*, 26–27.

14. Ibid., 36–39.

15. Ibid., 39–41.

16. Ibid., 42–43.

17. Henry Piddington, *The Sailor's Horn-Book for the Law of Storms....* (New York: John Wiley, 1848).

18. Donlin, *Furious Sky*, 46.

19. Other major cyclogenetic processes include extratropical cyclones, which tend to form along weather fronts, and of which a nor'easter is a well-known example, and mesocyclones, which tend to be localized within thunderstorms and sometimes spawn tornados or waterspouts. Tropical depressions and tropical storms are lesser forms of tropical cyclones.

20. Donlin, *Furious Sky*, xxi–xxiv.

21. In 1890, the Weather Bureau, as it was then known, moved from the War Department to the Department of Agriculture.

22. *Joint Resolution to Authorize the Secretary of War to Provide for Taking Meteorological Observations at the Military Stations and Other Points in the Interior of the Continent, and for Giving Notice on the Northern Lakes and Seaboard of the Approach and Force of Storms, Stats at Large of USA* 16 (1963): 369. This can be accessed online through the Library of Congress.

23. For a detailed overview of the 1893 and 1900 hurricanes, see Donlin, *Furious Sky*, 63–106.

24. National Academy of Sciences, *The National Academy of Sciences: The First Hundred Years 1863–1963* (Washington, D.C.: National Academies Press, 1978), 12. Available at www.ncbi.nlm.nih.gov.

25. Donlin, *Furious Sky*, 134.

26. John L. Frazier, "Storm Warnings—Hurricane Coming," *Honolulu Advertiser*, July 21, 1935.

27. For detailed accounts of the Labor Day Hurricane of 1935 see Willie Drye, *Storm of the Century: The Labor Day Hurricane of 1935*, rev. ed. (Guilford, CT: Lyons Press, 2019) and Willie Drye, "The True Story of the Most Intense Hurricane You've Never Heard Of," *National Geographic*, September 2017.

28. Donlin, *Furious Sky*, 174, 177.

29. Kneeland, *Playing Politics with Natural Disaster*, 15–16.

30. Ibid., 17–18.

31. R.H. Simpson and Arnold L. Sugg, *The Atlantic Hurricane Season of 1969* (Miami, FL: National Hurricane Center, National Weather Bureau, Environmental Science Services Administration, 1970), 298; Donlin, *Furious Sky*, 231–32; National Weather Service, "Hurricane Camille (1969): From Major Hurricane to Catastrophic Inland Flood," https://noaa.maps.arcgis.com; Lawrence Brown, "Flood '69: August 20–22," in *Flood '69: A Special Review of Camille's Visit to Virginia, A Keepsake Magazine* (Richmond, VA: Richmond Newspapers Inc., 1969); *Encyclopedia Virginia*, s.v. "Hurricane Camille (1969)."

32. "Camille," in *Flood '69: A Special Review of Camille's Visit to Virginia, A Keepsake Magazine* (Richmond, VA: U.S. Department of the Interior, 1970) [hereafter *Flood '69*], 5–7.

33. Brown, "Flood '69: August 20–22"; Lawrence Brown, "Death…and Irony"; and Bill Watson, "Missing: 16 Huffmans, 8 Perrys…," in *Flood '69*, 2.

34. National Weather Service Baltimore/Washington, "Hurricane Camille (1969): From Major Hurricane to Catastrophic Inland Flood." U.S. Department of the Interior, U.S. Geological Survey, *Debris-Flow Hazards within the Appalachian Mountains of the Eastern United States*, Fact Sheet 2008-3070, by Gerald F. Wieczorek and Benjamin A. Morgan, 2008; U.S. Department of Commerce, Environmental Science Services Administration, *The Virginia Floods, August 19–22, 1969: A Report to the Administrator*, September 1969, 1–2. U.S. Department of the Interior, *Flood of August 1969 in Virginia*, 7.

35. U.S. Department of Commerce, Environmental Science Services Administration, *Hurricane Camille: A Report to the Administrator*, September 1969, vi–viii.

36. U.S. Department of Commerce, *Virginia Floods*, v, 4–5.

37. Ibid., 6–9.

38. Ibid., 12–14.

2. CONDITIONS BEFORE AGNES

39. Virginia Department of Conservation and Recreation, Division of Natural Heritage, *Overview of the Physiography and Vegetation of Virginia*, 2021, 6.

40. Virginia Museum of History and Culture, "The Regions of Virginia," https://virginiahistory.org.

41. Virginia Department of Conservation and Recreation, *Overview of the Physiography and Vegetation*, 2–31.

42. Ibid., 9–10, 42; Virginia Museum of History and Culture, "Regions of Virginia."

43. Virginia Department of Conservation and Recreation, *Overview of the Physiography and Vegetation*, 37; Virginia Museum of History and Culture, "Regions of Virginia."

44. Meurine McLaughlin, "Arlandria's Dilemma: Floods, Buck-Passing," *Washington Post*, August 21, 1969.

45. Ibid.; "Around Town: Hope for Arlandria," *Washington Post*, July 13, 1970.

46. Some census records will show the town of Occoquan with a population of more than one thousand in 1970, an anomaly in sharp contrast to figures in the range of two to three hundred in every decennial census stretching back to 1860 and beginning again in 1980. The anomaly was apparently caused by a map error in the 1970 census that included a substantial number of residential units that were in fact outside of town boundaries. The issue came to light during the 1980 census and caused a considerable drop in town revenue from population-based distribution formulas. Mike Sager, "Occoquan Shrinks by 1,368," *Washington Post*, January 27, 1983.

47. Tom Nelson, *An Oral History: An Interview with Rosemary Selecman "Occoquan Friend"* (Occoquan, VA: Prince William County Historical Commission, 1980).

48. *Potomac News*, January 5, 1972; "New Site for Bridge?" *Potomac News*, May 10, 1972.

49. "Occoquan Bridge May Be Saved," *Potomac News*, June 7, 1972.

50. VSOCD Report—Department of Health After-Action Report: Report on Water Supplies and Waste Treatment Plants in Flooded Areas, 6.

51. Bob Rife, "In Vesuvius Flood Youth Drowns, 1 Missing," *Staunton Leader*, August 20, 1969; Bob Rife, "Area Death Toll at 2; Many Still Missing," *Staunton Leader*, August 21, 1969.

52. "Poor South River Channel Structure Blamed in Flood," *Staunton Leader*, August 22, 1969.

53. Jerry Lazarus, "After 39 Years, Salem Dam Project Debate Goes On," *Richmond Times-Dispatch*, March 20, 1972.

54. Ibid.

55. Ibid.; *Danville Register*, May 18, 1972.

56. James River Buffer Program, "The James River Watershed," https://www.jamesriverbuffers.org/the-james-river-watershed.html.

57. Brown, "Flood '69: August 20–22," *Flood '69*.

58. "Rampaging James Kills 12, Floods Towns and Bridges," *Farmville Herald*, August 22, 1969; "Eyewitness: Everybody Looked to Be Shocked," *Northern Virginia Sun*, August 22, 1969; "Godwin Explains Assistance Dispute," *Charlottesville Daily Progress*, August 29, 1969; "Waynesboro Flood Damage Now More Than $2 Million," *Waynesboro News-Virginian*, August 22, 1969; "Mennonites Praised for Nelson Efforts," *Waynesboro News-Virginian*, August 29, 1969; Joel Turner, "Buena Vista Residents Receive Relief Supplies," *Roanoke Times*, August 26, 1969.

59. "Town Council to Solve Speed, Noise Problems," *Farmville Herald*, June 21, 1972.

60. "State Plans Include Area Highway Projects," *Farmville Herald*, April 21, 1972.

61. "Powhatan News," *Farmville Herald*, April 5, 1972; "State Plans Include Area Highway Projects," *Farmville Herald*, April 21, 1972.

62. Ed Grimsley, "'Birthplace' of Richmond Now Appears Sick, Shaggy," *Richmond Times-Dispatch*, January 8, 1967.

63. Ed Grimsley, "Residents Say Fulton Bottom Can Be Saved," *Richmond Times-Dispatch*, January 15, 1972.

64. Christopher Silver, *Twentieth-Century Richmond: Planning, Politics, and Race* (Knoxville: University of Tennessee Press, 1984), 290, 297–98.

65. "JC's, Firemen Rescue Squad Join in Help," *Farmville Herald*, August 27, 1969.

66. Editorial, *Farmville Herald*, March 17, 1972; Robert S. Allen, "Senator Harry F. Byrd, Jr. Proposed Constitutional Change," *Farmville Herald*, March 22, 1972.

67. "County Democrats Meet Full Participation Rule," *Farmville Herald*, April 12, 1972; editorial, *Farmville Herald*, April 14, 1972.

68. "Town Voters Approve Bond Issue 929-59," *Farmville Herald*, March 3, 1972; "$109,783 Utility Extension Approved," *Farmville Herald*, April 14, 1972; "Construction Nears Two Million $ Mark," *Farmville Herald*, June 2, 1972; "State Plans Include Area Highway Projects," *Farmville Herald*, April 21, 1972.

69. "Prototype Civil Defense Plan Under Development," *Farmville Herald*, March 24, 1972; "New Commitment Made: Workable Civil Defense," *Farmville Herald*, April 28, 1972; "CAP Squadron Reactivated," *Farmville Herald*, April 28, 1972.

70. H.V. Lancaster, Jr., "National News Summary," *Farmville Herald*, June 21, 1972.

71. "37 Killed in Flooding in W. Va.," *Roanoke Times*, February 27, 1972; "Wildcat Strike Closes Mines in West Virginia," *Roanoke Times*, June 8, 1972.

72. Robert B. Sears, "Agnes's Blow Softened by Camille's Scars," *Roanoke Times*, August 3, 1972.

73. *Federal Civil Defense Act of 1950*, Public Law 920, 81st Congress (64 Stat. 1245). "Statement by the President Upon Signing the Federal Civil Defense Act of 1950, January 12, 1951," Harry S. Truman Presidential Library and Museum, https://www.trumanlibrary.gov/library/public-papers/10/statement-president-upon-signing-federal-civil-defense-act-1950 (accessed September 1, 2023).

74. Chapter 121, Civil Defense. 1952 Acts of General Assembly, H.B. No. 419. An Act to Amend and Reenact ## 44-141, 44-142, 44-144 and 44-145 of the Code of Virginia, Relating to Civilian Defense, and to Amend the Code of Virginia by Adding Eight New Sections Numbered ##44-142.1, 44-142.2, and 44-145.1 through 44-145.6 Relating to the Same Subject, and to Provide an Appropriation Therefor. Approved Feb. 25, 1952. Richmond: Virginia Office of Civilian Defense, 1952.

75. Stephen R. Fleming, "State Civil Defense Has New Mission," *Richmond Times-Dispatch*, May 28, 1972.

76. Commonwealth of Virginia, Office of Civil Defense, Office of the Governor, Natural Disaster Assistance Relief Plan, Richmond, Virginia, March 1972 (COVANDAP), foreword.

77. Stephen R. Fleming, "State Civil Defense Has New Mission," *Richmond Times-Dispatch*, May 28, 1972.

78. COVANDAP; Fleming, "State Civil Defense."

3. AGNES ARRIVES

79. "Agnes Nearly a Hurricane," *Tampa Tribune*, June 17, 1972; "Agnes Near Hurricane Force," *Orlando Evening Star*, June 17, 1972; "Hurricane's Tornados Hit Fla.," *Washington Post*, June 19, 1972.

80. Art Buchwald, "Stormy Women," *Washington Post*, April 27, 1972; National Hurricane Center and Central Pacific Hurricane Center, "Tropical Cyclone Naming History and Retired Names," www.nhc.noaa.gov.

81. "Agnes Nearly a Hurricane"; "Agnes Near Hurricane Force"; "Hurricane's Tornados Hit Fla."

82. William R. Amlong, "Agnes Spawns Vicious Tornados, Dies: At Least 5 Killed in Florida," *Miami Herald*, June 20, 1972; "Hurricane Dies," *Playground Daily News*, June 20, 1972.

83. Amlong, "Agnes Spawns Vicious Tornados."

84. Bill McNabb, "Agnes' Soaking Rains Save Georgia Crops," *Atlanta Constitution*, June 21, 1972.

85. Simpson and Herbert, *Atlantic Hurricane Season of 1972*, 328.

86. "Landslides, Floods Stun N.C. Mountain Families," *Charlotte Observer*, June 22, 1972.

87. A flood watch is issued when conditions are favorable for flooding; it does not mean that flooding will occur. A flood warning indicates the flood hazard is imminent or already occurring. National Weather Service, "Flood Warning vs. Watch," www.weather.gov.

88. VSOCD Report—Chronology: 06/20/72, 1310, 2000 (appears to be a typographical error labeling this entry "2100"), 2012, 2017, 2025.

89. VSOCD Report—Chronology: 06/20/72, 2037; Mike Steele and Bob Craig, "Evacuation Swift as the Water: Nelson Prepared for Agnes," *Charlottesville Daily Progress*, June 22, 1972. There is some modest discrepancy between the VSOCD report and press accounts regarding the timing and location of the evacuation centers. The subsequent press report makes no mention of the Woodson School in Lowesville but does mention the Roseland Rescue Squad, which the VSOCD report references the following day.

90. Ibid., 2340.

91. J.R. Schrader Jr., "Creek Changes Avert Tragedy," *Pulaski Southwest Times*, June 25, 1972.

92. "Agnes' Rains Deluge Locality: State Floods Close Roads; Residents Evacuate Homes," *Danville Bee*, June 21, 1972.

93. "Flood Waters Sweep Across Valley," *Radford News Journal*, June 21, 1972; Esther Williams, "Electricity Fails, Homes Evacuated," *Pulaski Southwest Times*, June 21, 1972; J.R. Schrader Jr., "Waters Receding but Not Very Fast," *Pulaski Southwest Times*, June 21, 1972.

94. "Flood Waters Sweep Across Valley," *Radford News Journal*, June 21, 1972; Esther Williams, "Electricity Fails, Homes Evacuated," *Pulaski Southwest Times*, June 21, 1972; J.R. Schrader Jr., "Waters Receding but Not Very Fast," *Pulaski Southwest Times*, June 21, 1972.

95. Esther Williams and J.R. Schrader Jr., "Flood Damages in Town Estimated at $300,000," *Pulaski Southwest Times*, June 22, 1972.

96. VSOCD Report—Chronology: 06/21/72, 2106.

97. Ben Beagle, "Flooding Forces Hundreds from Homes in Virginia: Property Damage Runs to Millions," *Roanoke Times*, June 22, 1972; Jim Shaver, "Flooding Forces Hundreds from Homes in Virginia: Flood in Valley Sets Record; River Crests at 19.35 Feet," *Roanoke Times*, June 22, 1972.

98. VSOCD Report—Department of Health After-Action Report, 33.

99. Beagle, "Flooding Forces Hundreds from Homes"; Shaver, "Flooding Forces Hundreds from Homes."

100. Shaver, "Flooding Forces Hundreds from Homes"; Frank Hancock, "Damage Put at Millions," *Roanoke World-News,* June 22, 1972.

101. "Looters and Sightseers Hamper Police Work," *Manassas Journal Messenger,* June 26, 1972.

102. J.R. Schrader Jr., "Waters Not Receding Very Fast," *Pulaski Southwest Times,* June 21, 1972.

103. "Warnings Issued," *Charlottesville Daily Progress,* June 22, 1972.

104. "Damage in County Tops $18 Million," *Potomac News,* June 26, 1972.

105. "Dangerous to Play Around Flood Waters," *Farmville Herald,* June 23, 1972; "National Guard Called Out," *Farmville Herald,* June 23, 1972; Ted Rohrlich, "'Snakes, Catfish' Hunted in Fulton," *Richmond Times-Dispatch,* June 24, 1972.

106. "Many Flirted with Death During Flood," *Roanoke World News,* June 22, 1972.

107. "Dangerous to Play Around Flood Waters."

108. Shaver, "Flooding Forces Hundreds from Homes."

109. Jenny Cook, "Flooded Stream Took Homes, Gardens, Cars," *Radford News Journal,* June 22, 1972.

110. VSOCD Report—Chronology: 06/21/72, 2030.

111. Ibid., 1215.

112. "Agnes' Rains Deluge Locality"; "Streams Go on Worst Rampage in 50 Years," *Danville Register,* June 22, 1972.

113. "Manassas Dam Break Kills Man," *Culpepper Star-Exponent,* June 22, 1972; VSOCD Report—Chronology: 06/21/72, 1322. This is again an example of an inconsistency between the VSOCD report and the press accounts.

114. VSOCD Report—Chronology: 06/21/72, 1215.

115. Ibid., 1205.

116. VSOCD Report—Overview.

117. Mike Steele and Bob Craig, "Evacuation Swift as the Water: Nelson Prepared for Agnes," *Charlottesville Daily Progress,* June 22, 1972.

118. VSOCD Report—Chronology: 06/21/72, 1326.

119. "Mail Went Through," *Charlottesville Daily Progress,* June 22, 1972.

120. VSOCD Report—Chronology: 06/21/72, 1327.

121. "Town's Worst Flood Is Major Disaster," *Farmville Herald,* June 23, 1972; "Flooded Plant Makes Water Supply Critical," *Farmville Herald,* June 23, 1972.

122. VSOCD Report—Chronology: 06/21/72, 1455, 1505.

123. VSOCD Report—Chronology: 06/21/72, 1648, 1740, 1748. This incident reflects the tragedy and confusion that can often surround deaths that occur during natural disasters. Initial reports alleged that there were

two children in the car and that the driver ignored roadblocks and drove into the floodwaters. But the individuals involved were in their sixties, and later reports do not mention any children. Additionally, the first name of one of the victims is mistaken in some reports, and the incident is listed as occurring variously in central Virginia, Appomattox County, Buchanan County, Buckingham County and Richmond County. Death certificate records, however, clearly indicate that the deaths occurred on Route 60 in Buckingham County near Brick Kiln Branch, a tributary of the James that Route 60 crosses. The death certificate and a marriage record from a few days later suggest that the couple may have been traveling to the wedding (the man was a minister) of their daughter in Fort Monroe, Virginia.

124. For a complete death toll and discussion of the ambiguity surrounding Virginia deaths associated with Agnes see Appendix II.

125. "Flood Situation in Brief," *Richmond Times Dispatch*, June 22, 1972; Lawrence Brown, "James Exceeding '69 Level; Damage Runs into Millions," June 23, 1972.

126. "Swirling Floodwaters Kill Three in Area; Scottsville Is Submerged," *Charlottesville Daily Progress*, June 22, 1972.

127. Ibid.; VSOCD—Chronology: 06/21/72, 2143.

128. Cathy Klarfeld, "Free Bridge Teetering: Belmont Homes Hit Hard," *Charlottesville Daily Progress*, June 22, 1972; Carol Harowitz, "Rec Center Evacuees Keep a Stiff Upper Lip," *Charlottesville Daily Progress*, June 22, 1972.

129. "Storm Leftovers Deluge 4 Counties with Floods," *Harrisonburg Daily News-Record*, June 22, 1972; "Residents On Guard as Deluge Continues," *Waynesboro News-Virginian*, June 21, 1972.

130. VSOCD Report—Chronology: 06/21/72, 1920.

131. Ed Berlin, "Grim Cleanup Job Under Way as Costly Flood Eases at Last: Homes, Stores Feel Brunt," *Waynesboro News-Virginian*, June 22, 1972.

132. VSOCD Report—Chronology: 06/21/72, 1518.

133. Ibid. The confusion was understandable. In the greater Waynesboro area, the communities of Waynesboro, Lyndhurst, Sherando and Stuart's Draft are in proximity.

134. Jerry Curtis, "Flooding Said Equal to That from Camille," *Waynesboro News-Virginian*, June 22, 1972.

135. Thelma Smith, "Flood Makes Ghost Town of City's Club Court Area," *Waynesboro News-Virginian*, June 22, 1972.

136. Ibid.

137. "Many Evacuated in County Areas," *Waynesboro News-Virginian*, June 22, 1972; "Cleanup Operations Under Way," *Staunton Leader*, June 22, 1972.

138. Garvey Winegar, "Fear of Coles Run Dam Break Brings Evacuation," *Waynesboro News-Virginian*, June 22, 1972.

139. VSOCD Report—Chronology: 06/21/1972, 1518, 1825.

140. Ed Berlin, "Grim Cleanup Job Underway as Costly Flood Eased at Last: Homes, Stores Feel Brunt," *Waynesboro News-Virginian*, June 22, 1972.

141. VSOCD Report—Chronology: 06/21/72, 1920.

142. "Storm Leftover Deluge 4 Counties with Floods," *Harrisonburg Daily News-Record*, June 22, 1972.

143. VSOCD Report—Chronology: 06/21/72, 1920.

144. "RR Wreck Averted by Prompt Action," *Orange Review*, June 29, 1972.

145. "Agnes Leaves State Areas Flooded," *Harrisonburg Daily News-Record*, June 22, 1972; "Havoc All Over State," *Charlottesville Daily Progress*, June 22, 1972; VSOCD Report—Chronology: 06/21/72, 2030; Kathleen Hoffman, "Heavy Rain Brings Record Flood to Area: Trailer Court is Evacuated," *Culpeper Star-Exponent*, June 22, 1972; Bo Prichard, "Family of 5 Rescued from Flooded Auto," *Culpeper Star-Exponent*, June 22, 1972.

146. Lulu Williams, "Local Streams Submerge Fields," *Winchester Evening Star*, June 22, 1972; "Front Royal Area Waiting for Crest, *Winchester Evening Star*, June 22, 1972; "May Be State's Worst," *Winchester Evening Star*, June 22, 1972; Nancy Pennypacker, "Rainfall Total Well Below 1942 Figure," *Winchester Evening Star*, June 22, 1972.

147. VSOCD Report—Chronology: 06/21/72, 1730, 1845, 1920, 1930, 2054, 2058.

148. "Agnes's Rains Deluge Locality"; "Dan River Crests at 20.9 Feet: Rainfall Over Eight Inches; Area Flooding Widespread," *Danville Bee*, June 22, 1972.

149. VSOCD Report—Chronology: 06/21/72, 1655, 1710.

150. Ibid., 1800.

151. "Families Evacuated in Nelson County Flooding," *Richmond Times-Dispatch*, June 21, 1972.

152. VSOCD Report—Chronology: 06/21/72, 1910; "Barcroft Danger Averted: Roads Blocked; Six Dead in Downstate Va.," *Washington Post*, June 22, 1972; Lawrence Brown, "Camille Outdone in Destruction: The State," *Richmond Times-Dispatch*, June 24, 1972.

153. VSOCD Report—Chronology: 06/21/72, 1930.

154. Marilyn Finley, "Flood Hits Western End Hard; 1,300 Refugees Flee Homes," *Potomac News*, June 23, 1972.

155. VSOCD Report—Chronology: 06/21/72, 2329, 2330.

156. Lawrence Brown, "6 Known Dead in Virginia as Flooding Intensifies," *Richmond Times Dispatch*, June 22, 1972.

157. Betty Calvin, "Flood Havoc Heavy," *Potomac* News, June 23, 1972; Marilyn Muse, "Botts Fire Station Was Occoquan's Refuge," *Potomac News*, June 23, 1972.

158. Calvin, "Flood Havoc Heavy"; Muse, "Botts Fire Station Was Occoquan's Refuge"; Eileen Mead, "The Calls for Help Were Many," *Potomac News*, June 26, 1972.

159. VSOCD Report—Chronology: 06/22/72, 0018, 031, 055.

160. Mead, "Calls for Help Were Many."

161. "Gov. Holton Delays Request for Disaster Area Status," *Roanoke Times*, June 23, 1972; Brown, "6 Known Dead."

162. "Barcroft Danger Averted: Roads Blocked; Six Dead in Downstate Va.," *Washington Post*, June 22, 1972.

163. Bart Barnes, "12,000 Evacuate Dwellings," *Washington Post*, June 23, 1972.

164. VSOCD Report—Chronology: 06/22/72, 0023.

165. "Barcroft Danger Averted"; Barnes, "12,000 Evacuate Dwellings.".

166. Finley, "Flood Hits Western End Hard."

167. "Flood Woes Give Hard Day's Night for Executive," *Potomac News*, June 23, 1972.

168. Finley, "Flood Hits Western End Hard."

169. Ibid.; Eileen Mead, "Neighbors Offer Food, Shelter to Flood Victims," *Potomac News*, June 23, 1972; "Flood Woes Give Hard Day's Night."

170. Finley, "Flood Hits Western End Hard."

171. VSOCD Report—Chronology: 06/22/72, 0001, 0010.

172. "Agnes Killed the Land, Spared People," *Charlottesville Daily Progress*, June 22, 1972.

173. "Flood Situation in Brief," *Richmond Times-Dispatch*, June 22, 1972.

174. Jerry Lazarus, "Would Salem Church Dam Have Curtailed Flooding," *Richmond Times-Dispatch*, June 26, 1972.

175. VSOCD Report—Chronology: 06/22/72, 0945.

176. "Dan River Crests at 20.9 Feet: Rainfall Over Eight Inches; Area Flooding Widespread," *Danville Bee*, June 22, 1972.

177. "South Boston Hard Hit by Flooding," *Danville Bee*, June 23, 1972.

178. VSOCD Report—Chronology: 06/22/72, 0655, 0945, 1020; 1045, 1155, 1320.

179. VSOCD Report—"Evaluation and Recommendations."

180. VSOCD Report—Division of Engineering and Buildings After-Action Report: Memorandum dated September 11, 1972, to Coordinator of State Office of Civil Defense from Director of the Division of Engineering and Buildings.

181. "Gov. Holton Delays Request."

182. Ibid.; VSOCD Report—Highlights (The report's "Overview" includes what appears to be a typographical error indicating the flight took place on "Thursday, June 23"; Thursday was June 22); Mike Grim, "Sight Was Nasty; People Said Little," *Richmond Times Dispatch*, June 23, 1972; Brown, "James Exceeding '69 Level."

183. "Power Goes Out in Fluvanna Area," *Charlottesville Daily Progress*, June 22, 1972.

184. M.R. Hornblower, "Governor Surveys Scottsville Damage," *Charlottesville Daily Progress*, June 22, 1972.

185. Betty Booker, "Power Cut Off in Fluvanna; Scottsville Calls It the Worst," *Charlottesville Daily Progress*, June 23, 1972.

186. Lulu Williams, "Local Streams Submerge Fields," *Winchester Evening Star*, June 22, 1972.

187. Doug O'Connell, "Storm's Rainfall 8 Inches Here," *Winchester Evening Star*, June 23, 1972.

188. David Smith, "Warren Is Called Disaster Area as Shenandoah Starts Receding," *Winchester Evening Star*, June 23, 1972.

189. "Clarke Houses Lost Along River Road," *Winchester Evening Star*, June 23, 1972.

190. "Front Royal Area Waiting for Crest," *Winchester Evening Star*, June 22, 1972.

191. O'Connell, "Storm's Rainfall 8 Inches Here."

192. Smith, "Warren Is Called Disaster Area."

193. VSOCD Report—Chronology: 06/22/72, 0335.

194. Wendy Migdal, "Retro Reads: Remembering Hurricane Agnes, 50 Years Later," *Fredericksburg Free Lance-Star*, June 23, 2022.

195. "Damage Estimates Set at $3.1 Million," *Richmond Times Dispatch*, June 28, 1972.

196. "James Gauges Out; Crests Estimated," *Richmond Times Dispatch*, June 23, 1972.

197. James E. Davis, "Flood Control Effort Took Planning, Work," *Richmond Times Dispatch*, June 23, 1972; "Richmond Orders Use of Flood Plan," *Richmond Times Dispatch*, June 22, 1972; James Berry, *The Richmond Flood* (Lubbock, TX: CF Boone, 1972), 5.

198. "Richmond Orders Use of Flood Plan," *Richmond Times Dispatch*, June 22, 1972; Stephen Fleming, "Cresting Due Here at 9 a.m. at Locks," *Richmond Times Dispatch*, June 23, 1972; Davis, "Flood Control Effort Took Planning."

199. James F. Bailey, James Lee Patterson and Joseph Louis Hornore Paulhus, *Hurricane Agnes Rainfall and Floods, June–July 1972*, Geological Survey Professional Paper 924, report prepared jointly by the U.S. Geological Survey and the National Oceanic and Atmospheric Administration, 68.

200. Accounts of when the bridge collapsed vary, even in those from the same day and the same source. The ambiguity is understandable, for even after the bridge buckled and became a tangle of iron, it was still some time before it washed away. Accordingly, while one account says 10:30 a.m., for example, another says early afternoon. Betty Calvin, "Flood Havoc Heavy," *Potomac News*, June 23, 1972; "Goodbye, Old Friend," *Potomac News*, June 23, 1972.

201. VSOCD Report—Chronology: 6/22/72, 1630; "Belvoir Troops Saw Flood Action," *Potomac News*, June 28, 1972; "Weakened Dam Menaces Virginia Town; 5 Dead," *Roanoke Times*, June 23, 1972.

202. "Man Drowns in Trailer Parking Lot," *Potomac News*, June 23, 1972.

203. Charlie Hines, "Drama at Neabsco Creek," *Potomac News*, June 23, 1972.

204. Mead, "Neighbors Offer Food."

205. "Gov. Holton Delays Request"; Finley, "Flood Hits Western End Hard."

206. Roger Miller, "Plane Said Down in Swollen James," *Charlottesville Daily Progress*, June 24, 1972.

207. VSOCD—Report: Chronology: 06/22/72, 1618, 1745; Dan Richards and Bo Prichard, "Culpeper Is Declared 'Disaster' Area: Adjoining Counties Included," *Culpeper Star-Exponent*, June 24, 1972.

208. VSOCD Report—Chronology: 06/22/23, 2058 (refers in that entry to later reports at 2210, and on 06/23/72 at 0110).

209. Shelley Rolfe, "Holton Awaits Firm Flood Date Before Asking U.S. Aid," *Richmond Times-Dispatch*, June 23, 1972.

210. VSOCD Report—Overview. VSOCD Report—Highlights.

211. VSOCD Report—Chronology: 06/22/72, 1010, 1315, 1415, 1650, 1720, 1905, 2015.

212. Brown, "James Exceeding '69 Level"; VSOCD Report—Chronology: 06/22/72, 2120; Brown, "6 Known Dead."

213. VSOCD Report—Chronology: 06/22/72, 1630, 1230; VSOCD Report—Chronology: 06/23/72, 0310, 1148.

214. "Flooded Plant Makes Water Supply Critical," *Farmville Herald*, June 23, 1972; VSOCD Report—Chronology: 06/22/72, 2130.

215. "Many 'New' Areas Affected," *Richmond Times-Dispatch*, June 23, 1972.

216. VSOCD Report—Chronology: 06/22/92, 2324.

217. VSOCD Report—Chronology: 06/23/72, 0137; Stephen Fleming, "Cresting Due Here at 9 a.m. At Locks," *Richmond Times Dispatch,* June 23, 1972.

218. Fleming, "Cresting Due Here at 9 a.m. At Locks"; Stephen Fleming, "Camille Outdone in Destruction: The Area," *Richmond Times-Dispatch*, June 24, 1972; Davis, "Flood Control Effort."

219. Ted Rohrlich, "Shockoe Frenetic; Fulton Waited," *Richmond Times-Dispatch*, June 23, 1972; Davis, "Flood Control Effort Took Planning"; Rohrlich, "'Snakes, Catfish' Hunted"; Fleming, "Camille Outdone in Destruction"; VSOCD Report—Chronology: 06/23/72, 1230.

220. David M. Howe, "South Bank Peril Slight," *Richmond Times-Dispatch*, June 23, 1972; David M. Howe, "Tanks Shift, Threatening Oil Spill Here," *Richmond Times-Dispatch*, June 24, 1972; VSOCD Report—Chronology: 06/23/72, 1310.

221. Fleming, "Camille Outdone in Destruction"; VSOCD Report—Chronology: 06/23/72, 0600, 0806; James N. Woodson, "Dry Spigots Are Expected Today," *Richmond Times-Dispatch,* June 24, 1972.

222. VSOCD Report—Chronology: 06/23/72, 1330.

223. VSOCD Report—Proclamation by the Governor of Virginia: Emergency Proclamation, June 23, 1972; James Latimer, "Two-Thirds of State Will Receive U.S. Aid," *Richmond Times-Dispatch*, June 24, 1972; Governor Linwood Holton to General George A. Lincoln, June 23, 1972 (available in VSOCD Report).

224. Latimer, "Two-Thirds of State"; Brown, "Camille Outdone in Destruction"; VSOCD Report—Chronology: 06/23/72, 1450; "Culpepper Is Declared 'Disaster Area': 25 Cities, 63 Counties Listed," *Culpeper Star-Exponent,* June 24, 1972.

225. VSOCD Report—Highlights.

226. Latimer, "Two-Thirds of State Will Receive U.S. Aid"; VSOCD Report—Chronology: 06/23/72, 1600, 1845.

227. VSOCD Report—Chronology: 06/30/72, 1405, 2340.

228. Fleming, "Camille Outdone in Destruction"; VSOCD Report—National Weather Service Provisional Crest Data.

229. Miller, "Plane Said Down."

230. Brown, "Camille Outdone in Destruction"; Claude Burrows, "Many Motorists Get Unexpected City Tour," *Richmond Times-Dispatch,* June 24, 1972.

231. Fleming, "Cresting Due Here at 9 a.m."; Hilliard, "Counties Are Surprised by Flood," *Richmond Times Dispatch,* June 24, 1972.

4. RECOVERY AND ASSESSMENT

232. VSOCD Report—Highlights.
233. VSOCD Report—Chronology: 06/24/2023, 0030, 2025; James Ezzell, "Cutter Fought the Flooding James to Free Trapped Barge at Dutch Gap," *Richmond Times Dispatch*, June 25, 1972.
234. Ezzell, "Cutter Fought the Flooding James."
235. VSOCD Report—Chronology: 06/24/72, 1200.
236. Brown, "Camille Outdone in Destruction."
237. "River, Creek Floods Watched," *Petersburg Progress-Index*, June 22, 1972.
238. "Petersburg Unlikely to Have Flooding," *Richmond Times-Dispatch*, June 27, 1972; "River Crest 16' Feet Tonight," *Petersburg Progress-Index*, June 26, 1972; "River Crests, Little Flooding," *Petersburg Progress-Index*, June 27, 1972.
239. Bart Barnes, "12,000 Evacuate Dwellings," *Washington Post*, June 23, 1972.
240. VSOCD Report—Chronology: 06/24/72, 0910, 1340, 1825, 1830; VSOCD Report—Chronology: 06/26/72, 1320.
241. Hilliard, "Counties Are Surprised by Flood."
242. Brown, "Camille Outdone in Destruction"; "Many 'New' Areas Affected," *Richmond Times-Dispatch*, June 23, 1972; Brown, "James Exceeding '69 Level"; Lawrence Brown, "West End, North Side Are Dry," *Richmond Times Dispatch*, June 25, 1972.
243. "N. Virginia Has Water Crisis in Flood Wake," *Washington Post*, June 23, 1972.
244. "About 3,000 Received Weekend Tetanus Shots," *Manassas Journal Messenger*, June 26, 1972; "Explorer Groups Work with Area Rescue Squads," *Potomac News*, June 28, 1972.
245. VSOCD Report—Department of Health After-Action Report, 5.
246. "No Plans Made for Vaccinations," *Richmond Times-Dispatch*, June 25, 1972.
247. VSOCD Report—Department of Health After-Action Report, 12.
248. Hilliard, "Counties Are Surprised by Flood."
249. Bill Wall, "Unbelievable, Overwhelming Aid Returns Town to Normal," *Farmville Herald*, June 28, 1972.
250. Brown, "West End, North Side."
251. Fleming, "Camille Outdone in Destruction."
252. James N. Woodson, "Dry Spigots Are Expected Today," *Richmond Times-Dispatch*, June 24, 1972.
253. James N. Woodson, "Water May Be Restored Today," *Richmond Times-Dispatch*, June 25, 1972.

254. Woodson, "Dry Spigots Are Expected"; Laurence Hilliard, "Worst Is Over in Henrico, Chesterfield," *Richmond Times-Dispatch*, June 25, 1972.

255. Jann Malone, "Few Richmonders Thirsty Until the Taps Run Dry," *Richmond Times-Dispatch*, June 25, 1972.

256. Brown, "West End, North Side"; Woodson, "Dry Spigots Are Expected."

257. Woodson, "Water May Be Restored Today"; Laurence Hilliard, "Henrico Should Get Water This Morning," *Richmond Times-Dispatch*, June 27, 1972.

258. Woodson, "Water May Be Restored."

259. Jann Malone, "Water Seekers Flock to Willow Lawn," *Richmond Times-Dispatch*, June 26, 1972.

260. David D. Ryan, "Misuse of Scarce Water Brings Quick Crackdowns," *Richmond Times-Dispatch*, June 27, 1972.

261. "City Asks Firms Using Much Water to Close," *Richmond Times-Dispatch*, June 26, 1972.

262. Shelly Rolfe, "Water Shortage Provides Lesson in Cooperation," *Richmond Times-Dispatch*, June 25, 1972.

263. Woodson, "Water May Be Restored."

264. David D. Ryan, "Water Again Flows in City Mains," *Richmond Times-Dispatch*, June 26, 1972.

265. Ibid.; Ryan, "Misuse of Scarce Water."

266. Ryan, "Water Again Flows."

267. Ryan, "Misuse of Scarce Water"

268. "City Asks Firms Using Much Water to Close," *Richmond Times-Dispatch*, June 26, 1972.

269. "Water System Now Normal," *Richmond Times-Dispatch*, June 30, 1972.

270. "Repairs Underway at Plant," *Potomac News*, June 26, 1972; Brown, "West End, North Side."

271. Betty Calvin, "Flood Havoc Heavy: Three Drown, Water Supply Disrupted," *Potomac News*, June 23, 1972; "N. Virginia Has Water Crisis in Flood Wake," *Washington Post*, June 23, 1972.

272. Marilyn Finley, "Water, Water Everywhere but Little of It to Drink," *Potomac News*, June 26, 1972.

273. VSOCD Report—Department of Health After-Action Report, 10–14.

274. Calvin, "Flood Havoc Heavy"; "N. Virginia Has Water Crisis in Flood Wake," *Washington Post*, June 23, 1972.

275. VSOCD Report—Department of Health After-Action Report, 10–14.

276. "Repairs Underway at Plant," *Potomac News*, June 26, 1972.

277. Eileen Mead, "The Calls for Help Were Many," *Potomac News*, June 26, 1972.

278. "Repairs Underway at Plant," *Potomac News*, June 26, 1972.

279. "Long Outage Seen for Two Stations," *Richmond Times-Dispatch*, June 27, 1972.

280. Roger Miller, "Power Cut Off in Fluvanna; Scottsville Call It the Worst: Fluvanna," *Charlottesville Daily Progress*, June 23, 1972; Brown, "West End, North Side."

281. VSOCD Report—Chronology: 06/26/72—06/29/72, 2325. The chronology fails to provide headings indicating the days between June 24 and June 27, but the 24 hour time format used enables identification of the specific day.

282. "Riverside Dr. Stores Ready for Business," *Danville Bee*, June 23, 1972.

283. Brown, "Camille Outdone in Destruction"; "Post-Flood Cleanup Underway as River Returns to Banks," *Danville Bee*, June 24, 1972.

284. Brown, "Camille Outdone in Destruction."

285. Ibid.; Brown, "West End, North Side."

286. Wendy Midgal, "Retro Reads: Remembering Hurricane Agnes, 50 Years Later," *Fredericksburg Free Lance-Star*, June 23, 2022.

287. "Big Cleanup Gets Underway," *Potomac News*, June 26, 1972.

288. Marilyn Muse, "Occoquan Fights Back: At 10-Yard-Line and Punting," *Potomac News*, June 26, 1972.

289. Dave Lynch, "VFW Found Comrades in Distress," letter to the editor, *Potomac* News, June 28, 1972.

290. "Explorer Groups Work with Area Rescue Squads," *Potomac News*, June 28, 1972.

291. Ann Holiday and Kevin Murphy, "Occoquan Begins Tremendous Task of Restoration," *Manassas Journal Messenger*, June 26, 1972; Mead, "Calls for Help Were Many"; Muse, "Occoquan Fights Back." The reported number of volunteers from Lake Ridge varies significantly between these three sources, even among different articles from the same newspaper. Whereas the *Potomac News* reports 150 in one story and 100 in another, the *Manassas Journal Messenger* reports 70. In the text, I settle for a range between the two lower figures as the most likely.

292. "City and County: Officials Thank Students," *Charlottesville Daily Progress*, June 29, 1972.

293. "Mennonites Aid in City Cleanup," *Richmond Times-Dispatch*, June 29, 1972.

294. "City Helps Self, Others During Flood," *Charlottesville Daily Progress*, July 3, 1972.

295. "Godwin Explains Assistance Dispute," *Charlottesville Daily Progress*, August 29, 1969.

296. VSOCD Report—Chronology: 06/23/72, 1330.

297. Alan Cooper, "Damage to Key Industry Seen as Costly to Scottsville," *Richmond Times-Dispatch*, June 25, 1972.

298. VSOCD Report—Chronology: 06/24/72, 1340.

299. Ibid., 1825.

300. "Holton Bars Cleanup by Units of Guard," *Richmond Times-Dispatch*, June 28, 1972.

301. VSOCD Report—Chronology: 06/26/72, 1700, 2030.

302. Brown, "Camille Outdone in Destruction."

303. "Speedy Aid Promised," *Charlottesville Daily Progress*, June 26, 1972.

304. VSOCD Report—Highlights.

305. James Latimer, "Virginians May Expect Prompt Help," *Richmond Times-Dispatch*, June 25, 1972; "Business, Farm, Lost Pay Financial Aid Now Flowing," *Farmville Herald*, June 28, 1972; "Federal Flood Assistance Sought by Area Residents," *Potomac News*, July 5, 1972; "Post-Flood Cleanup Underway as River Returns to Banks," *Danville Bee*, June 24, 1972.

306. "Water System Now Normal," *Richmond Times-Dispatch*, June 30, 1972.

307. See e.g., "Disaster Loan," *Staunton News-Leader*, July 9, 1972.

308. "Repayment of Loans from '69 Suspended," *Richmond Time-Dispatch*, July 6, 1972.

309. William H. Jones, "Md., Va. Preparing to Seek U.S. Relief," *Washington Post*, June 23, 1972.

310. "Officials Outline Flood Relief Progress," *Potomac News*, July 12, 1972.

311. William H. Jones, "Md., Va. Preparing to Seek U.S. Relief," *Washington Post*, June 23, 1972; Mike Grim, "City Thought to Fear Flood Coverage Effects," *Richmond Times-Dispatch*, July 1, 1972.

312. Mike Grim, "An Overview: Sight Was Nasty; People Said Little," *Richmond Times-Dispatch*, June 23, 1972.

313. Mike Grim, "City Thought to Fear Flood Coverage Effects, *Richmond Times-Dispatch*, July 1, 1972.

314. Ibid.

315. Stephen Fleming, "Flood Victims Rounded Up for Visitor," *Richmond Times-Dispatch*, June 29, 1972.

316. Mike Grim, "Flood Study Cites City on Insurance," *Richmond Times-Dispatch*, January 18, 1973.

317. Lazarus, "Would Salem Church Dam."

318. Joel Turner, "Floodplain Restrictions: Is It Already Too Late?" *Roanoke Times*, March 18, 1973; Joe Gilliland, "Roanoke Planner Fears Floodplain Expansion," *Roanoke Times*, March 18, 1973.

319. "The Receding Waters," opinion, *Potomac News*, June 26, 1972.
320. "$3 to $4 Millions Flood Damage Seen: River Depth Tops 1940 Mark 5 Feet," *Farmville Herald*, June 28, 1972.
321. Ted Rohrlich, "Everyone Got into Cleanup Act," *Richmond Times-Dispatch*, July 2, 1972.
322. Mike Grim, "Flooded Merchants Plan Suit," *Richmond Times-Dispatch*, June 29, 1972.
323. "Bottom Resident Disgusted," *Richmond Times-Dispatch*, June 26, 1972.
324. Sid Cassese, "Shelter Still Needed for Fulton Victims," *Richmond Times-Dispatch*, June 29, 1972.
325. Jann Malone, "Fulton Residents 'Just Wait,' but They Win Housing Action," *Richmond Times-Dispatch*, July 1, 1972.
326. Sid Cassese, "Fulton Discussion Produces Please, Speech, Sudden End," *Richmond Times-Dispatch*, July 7, 1972.
327. Shelley Rolfe, "Agnew Views Damage, Lauds Civil Defense," *Richmond Times-Dispatch*, June 29, 1972.
328. VSOCD Report—Evaluation and Recommendations.
329. Brown, "6 Known Dead"; James N. Woodson, "Governor Wants All State Offices to Be Open Tomorrow If Possible," *Richmond Times-Dispatch*, June 25, 1972.
330. VSOCD Report—Evaluation and Recommendations.
331. Ibid.
332. *Natural Disaster Survey Report 73-1: Final Report of the Disaster Survey Team on the Events of Agnes*, National Oceanic and Atmospheric Administration, NDSR 73-1, 1.
333. VSOCD Report—Evaluation and Recommendations.
334. VSOCD Report—Division of Engineering and Buildings After-Action Report: Memorandum dated September 11, 1972, to Coordinator of State Office of Civil Defense from Director of the Division of Engineering and Buildings.
335. VSOCD Report—Department of Military Affairs After-Action Report, 7–9.
336. Robert B. Sears, "Agnes's Blow Softened by Camille's Scars," *Roanoke Times*, August 3, 1972.
337. VSOCD Report—Statistical and Damage Data as of July 20, 1972.
338. Brown, "6 Known Dead."
339. VSOCD Report—Statistical and Damage Data as of July 20, 1972. VSOCD Report—Department of Education After-Action Report: Counties and Cities in the Commonwealth of Virginia Reporting School Damage as a Result of Tropical Storm Agnes.

340. VSOCD Report—Department of Agriculture and Commerce After-Action Report: Letter from Mr. A. Lee Turner to Ray E. Vanhuss, Jr., September 6, 1972. VSOCD Report—Department of Agriculture and Commerce After-Action Report: Food Distribution Services: Tropical Storm Agnes. Activities Through June 28, 1972.

341. "Farmers List $6.6 Million Lost," *Richmond Times-Dispatch*, July 1, 1972; Laurence Hilliard, "Damage Could Be as High as $330 Million," *Richmond Times-Dispatch*, July 2, 1972.

342. "Fresh-Water Influx Hits Already Imperiled Oysters," *Richmond Times-Dispatch*, June 24, 1972.

343. "Shellfish Disaster Goes to OEP," *Charlottesville Daily Progress*, July 28, 1972; *Impact of Tropical Storm Agnes on Chesapeake Bay* (Baltimore: U.S. Army Corps of Engineers, 1975), 27.

5. AFTERMATH

344. U.S. Army Corps of Engineers, "Hurricane Agnes: Fifty Years Later," July 2022, www.usace.army.mil.

345. Kneeland, *Playing Politics with Natural Disaster*, 18–24.

346. Ibid.

347. Ibid., 65.

348. Richard Nixon, "Message to Congress Proposing Additional Disaster Relief Measures Following Tropical Storm Agnes," July 17, 1972. Available through the American Presidency Project at https://www.presidency.ucsb.edu.

349. "Hearing to Provide Additional Relief to the Victims of Hurricane and Tropical Storm Agnes, and to the Victims of the South Dakota Flood Disaster," Committee on Banking and Currency, U.S. House of Representatives, July 20, 1972; Kneeland, *Playing Politics with Natural Disaster*, 65–71.

350. Kneeland, *Playing Politics with Natural Disaster*, 65–71.

351. Richard Nixon Foundation, *Dealing with Disaster: 50 Years After Hurricane Agnes*, Richard Nixon Foundation, September 8, 2022, https://www.nixonfoundation.org.

352. Kneeland, *Playing Politics with Natural Disaster*, 75.

353. Ibid., 90, 135.

354. Commonwealth of Virginia Emergency Services and Disaster Law of 1973, *Acts and Joint Resolutions of the General Assembly of the Commonwealth of Virginia*, Session 1973, 339-346.

355. Kneeland, *Playing Politics with Natural Disaster*, 112–13, 141–45.

356. Ibid., 126–28.

357. U.S. Army Corps of Engineers, *Impact of Tropical Storm Agnes*, 15–17.

358. Ibid., 19–22.

359. Ibid., 18–19. Privately leased bars had higher mortality rates everywhere, which was attributed to their less favorable locations relative to freshwater discharge.

360. "State Highways Back to Normal After Flooding," *Richmond Times-Dispatch*, July 14, 1972; Claude Burrows, "State Is Penalized for Efficiency," *Richmond Times-Dispatch*, November 26, 1972.

361. "Flood-Damaged Cars Sold to Unsuspecting Buyers," *Roanoke Times*, July 25, 1972.

362. Marilyn Finley, "Flood Victims 'Taken?'" *Potomac News*, August 18, 1972.

363. VSOCD Report—Department of Health After-Action Report, 31–32.

364. "Artillery Brought in for 'Skeeter' War," *Staunton News-Leader*, August 2, 1972.

365. Roger Miller, "'Funny Looking Rocks': The Great Minie Ball Mystery," *Charlottesville Daily Progress*, July 22, 1972.

366. "Bridge Wreckage Sought by Divers," *Potomac News*, July 19, 1972.

367. Douglas Dilley, "Occoquan's Travail: A New Bridge?" *Potomac News*, July 12, 1972; "Bridge Projects Occupy Officials, *Potomac News*, August 12, 1972.

368. "North Bridge Falls; South May Reopen," *Potomac News*, July 21, 1972.

369. Marilyn Finley and Cyndi Young, "Agnes Revisited: Remnants of Devastation Still Apparent in County," *Potomac News*, June 20, 1973; Caron McConnon, "Business: Recovery and Death," *Potomac News*, June 20, 1973; Eileen Mead, "6.77 Inches of Rain in 24 Hours," *Potomac News*, September 26, 1975. In fact, just a few weeks after Agnes, heavy rains caused flash flooding in Occoquan from the same stream, and the developer of the nearby Lake Ridge community was reportedly trying to build some small holding ponds to control runoff. "Various Agencies Help Occoquan Recuperate," *Potomac News*, July 5, 1972.

370. Anne Hazard, "On a Bed of Bricks: Occoquan Resident Worries about Town's Next Flood," *Potomac News*, July 30, 1976; "Board Funds Only Half of Ballywhack Branch Work," *Potomac News*, February 10, 1977.

371. Finley and Young, "Agnes Revisited"; McConnon, "Business."

372. "Proposals for Dam Becomes Reality in Encyclopedia Britannica," *Newport News Daily Press*, August 18, 1988.

373. Larry Markley, "Water Rising Rapidly in Scottsville Again," *Richmond Times-Dispatch*, June 22, 1972.

374. Peter Bacque, "A Year Later, Scottsville Rebuilding Continues," *Charlottesville Daily Progress*, June 21, 1972.

375. *Richmond Times-Dispatch*, September 20, 1977.

376. Monte Basgall, "Bridge Loss Strangling Hamlet," *Richmond Times-Dispatch*, July 17, 1972; "Temporary Ferry Seen as Span Replacement," *Richmond Times-Dispatch*, July 20, 1972.

377. Bryan McKenzie, "Resigned to Reversion," *Charlottesville Daily Progress*, February 7, 2016.

378. Silver, *Twentieth-Century Richmond*, 306.

EPILOGUE

379. Dolin, *Furious Sky*, xxi.

SELECTED BIBLIOGRAPHY

One of the significant primary sources used was the Virginia State Office of Civil Defense *Report on Tropical Storm Agnes*, dated September 15, 1972. The report contains a variety of documents, including an overview, some daily highlights, a personnel roster, typed and handwritten statistical compilations of damages, evaluations and recommendations and after-action reports from state agencies and quasi-public and private organizations. Most valuable is a chronological history taken from actual emergency message forms and the logs kept by personnel at the emergency operations center from the afternoon of Tuesday, June 20, 1972, until Thursday, June 29, 1972. Most of the report is unpaginated. Consequently, to aid the reader in finding the source material in the notes I have adopted a convention for the report that characterizes it as "VSOCD Report" followed by a description of the section (e.g., Overview, Chronology). For material from the Chronology section of the report, I include the date in mm/dd/yy format, as well as the time record, the latter of which is recorded in twenty-four-hour display. For example, an entry in the chronology for June 29 at 10:15 a.m. would read as follows in the notes: VSOCD Report—Chronology: 06/29/72, 1015.

There are a wide variety of secondary sources available about hurricanes, only a few of which I have included here. For the chapter on the history and science of hurricanes, however, I specifically want to highlight Eric Jay Dolin's *A Furious Sky*, which is an excellent source readily available and accessible to the general reader, and on which I drew heavily for that particular chapter.

ARCHIVES

Commonwealth of Virginia, Office of Civil Defense, Office of the Governor. *Natural Disaster Assistance Relief Plan.* Richmond, Virginia, March 1972 (COVANDAP).

The Library of Virginia, Richmond, Virginia

Records of the Virginia Governor's Office, 1948, 1970–1985. Governor Linwood Holton, 1972.

Richmond Newspapers, Inc. *Floods '69: A Special Review of Camille's Visit to Virginia. A Keepsake Magazine.* August 1969. Found in Frank D. Johnson Papers, 1929–1986.

Virginia State Office of Civil Defense. *Report on Tropical Storm Agnes.* September 15, 1972.

PUBLISHED GOVERNMENT DOCUMENTS

Agnes in Virginia, June 1972. Norfolk: U.S. Army Corps of Engineers, Norfolk District, 1974.

Andersen, Aven Mayer, and William Jackson Davis. *Effects of Hurricane Agnes on the Environment and Organisms of the Chesapeake Bay; Early Findings and Recommendations. A Report for the U.S. Army Corps of Engineers.* Solomons, MD: U.S. Army Corps of Engineers, Philadelphia District, 1973.

Bailey, James, F., James Lee Patterson and Joseph Louis Hornore Paulhus. *Hurricane Agnes Rainfall and Floods, June–July 1972.* Geological Survey Professional Paper 924. Report prepared jointly by the U.S. Geological Survey and the National Oceanic and Atmospheric Administration, 1975.

Davis, Jackson. *The Effects of Tropical Storm Agnes on the Chesapeake Bay Estuarine System: Appendix [to] Impact of Tropical Storm Agnes on Chesapeake Bay.* Baltimore: U.S. Army Corps of Engineers, Baltimore District, 1975.

Impact of Tropical Storm Agnes on Chesapeake Bay. Baltimore: U.S. Army Corps of Engineers, Baltimore District, 1975.

National Hurricane Center and Central Pacific Hurricane Center. "Tropical Cyclone Naming History and Retired Names." www.nhc.noaa.gov.

National Oceanic and Atmospheric Administration. *The Agnes Floods: A Post-Audit of the Effectiveness of the Storm and Flood Warning System of the National Oceanic and Atmospheric Administration; a Report for the Administrator of NOAA.* Washington, 1972.

———. "50th Anniversary of Hurricane Agnes." https://agnes50-noaa. hub.arcgis.com.

———. *Natural Disaster Survey Report 73-1*. 1973.

National Weather Service. "Flood of June 1972 - Hurricane Agnes." www. weather.gov.

———. "Hurricane Agnes: June 19–24, 1972." www.weather.gov/ctp/Agnes.

———. "Hurricane Camille (1969): From Major Hurricane to Catastrophic Inland Flood." https://noaa.maps.arcgis.com.

Simpson, R.H., and Arnold L. Sugg. *The Atlantic Hurricane Season of 1969*. National Hurricane Center, National Weather Bureau, Environmental Science Services Administration. Miami, April 1970.

Simpson, R.H., and Paul J. Hebert. *Atlantic Hurricane Season of 1972*. National Hurricane Center, National Weather Service, NOAA. Miami, April 1973.

Tropical Storm Agnes. Washington: U.S. Army Corps of Engineers, 1973.

Tropical Storm Agnes, June 1972: Basins of the Susquehanna and Potomac Rivers and Maryland Portions of Chesapeake Bay and Atlantic Coast: Post Flood Report. Baltimore: U.S. Army Corps of Engineers, Baltimore District, 1975.

U.S. Army Corp of Engineers. "Hurricane Agnes: Fifty Years Later." www. usace.army.mil.

U.S. Congress. House of Representatives. Committee on Banking and Currency. *To Provide Additional Relief to the Victims of Hurricane and Tropical Storm Agnes, and to the Victims of the South Dakota Flood Disaster: Hearing on H.R. 15935*. 92 Congress, 2nd sess., July 20, 1972.

U.S. Congress. House of Representatives. Committee on Banking, Finance, and Urban Affairs. *Aftermath of Hurricane Agnes: field hearing before the Subcommittee on Policy Research and Insurance of the Committee on Banking, Finance, and Urban Affairs*, 101st Congress, 2nd sess., June 22, 1990.

U.S. Department of Commerce. *Hurricane Camille: August 14–22, 1969, Preliminary Report*. September 1969.

———. *Hurricane Camille: A Report to the Administrator*. September 1969.

———. *The Virginia Floods, August 19–22, 1969: A Report to the Administrator*. September 1969.

U.S. Department of the Interior. *Flood of August 1969 in Virginia*. Richmond, 1970.

U.S. Department of the Interior. U.S. Geological Survey. *Debris-Flow Hazards within the Appalachian Mountains of the Eastern United States* by Gerald F. Wieczorek and Benjamin A. Morgan. Fact Sheet 2008-3070. 2008. https://pubs.usgs.gov.

U.S. Natural Resources Conservation Service, and U.S National Cartography and Geospatial Center. *Completed River Basin Studies, Virginia: October*. [Fort Worth, Tex.: USDA-NRCS, National Cartography & Geospatial Center; Richmond, Va.: State Conservationist, distributor, 1998] Map. https://www.loc.gov.

U.S. Soil Conservation Service. *Administrative Areas Virginia*. Washington, D.C.: U.S. Department of Agriculture, Soil Conservation Service, 1987. Map. https://www.loc.gov/item.

U.S Soil Conservation Service, and U.S. National Cartographic Center. Major land resource areas MLRA by physiographic regions, January 1, Virginia. Ft. Worth, TX: USDA-SCS-National Cartographic Center; Richmond, Va.: State Conservationist, distributor, 1984. Map. https://www.loc.gov.

OTHER PRIMARY SOURCES

Nelson, Tom. *An Oral History: An Interview with Rosemary Selecman "Occoquan Friend."* Occoquan, VA: Prince William County Historical Commission, 1980.

Serow, William J., and Michael A. Spar. *Virginia's Population: A Decade of Change. [I] Demographic Profile*. Charlottesville: Bureau of Population and Economic Research, Graduate School of Business Administration, University of Virginia, 1972.

NEWSPAPERS

Charlottesville (VA) Daily Progress
Culpeper (VA) Star-Exponent
Danville (VA) Bee
Danville (VA) Register
Farmville (VA) Herald
Harrisonburg (VA) Daily News-Record
Manassas (VA) Journal Messenger
Newport News (VA) Daily Press
Northern Virginia Sun (Falls Church, VA)
Orange (VA) Review
Petersburg (VA) Progress-Index
Potomac News (Woodbridge, VA)

Pulaski (VA) Southwest Times
Radford (VA) News Journal
Richmond (VA) Times-Dispatch
Roanoke (VA) Times
Roanoke (VA) World-News
Staunton (VA) News-Leader
Washington Post (Washington, D.C.)
Waynesboro (VA) News Virginian
Winchester (VA) Evening Star

SECONDARY SOURCES

Barnhart, Robert K., ed. *The Barnhardt Concise Dictionary of Etymology*. New York: HarperCollins Publishers, Inc., 1995.

Cox, Jeremy. "50 Years Later: Killer Storm Agnes Continues to Haunt Chesapeake Bay Watershed." *Bay Journal*, June 21, 2022. www.bayjournal.com.

Dolin, Eric Jay. *A Furious Sky: The Five Hundred-Year History of America's Hurricanes*. New York: Liveright Publishing Corporation, 2020.

Drye, Willie. *Storm of the Century: The Labor Day Hurricane of 1935*. Rev. ed. Guilford, CT: Lyons Press, 2019.

———. "The True Story of the Most Intense Hurricane You've Never Heard Of." *National Geographic*, September 2017.

Green, Paula F. *The Great Virginia Flood of 1870*. Charleston, SC: The History Press, 2020.

Kneeland, Timothy W. *Playing Politics with Natural Disaster: Hurricane Agnes, the 1972 Election, and the Origins of FEMA*. Ithaca, NY: Cornell University Press, 2020.

National Academy of Sciences. "The New Deal and the Science Advisory Board." In *The National Academy of Sciences: The First Hundred Years 1863– 1963*, 347–81. Washington, D.C.: National Academies Press, 1978.

Richard Nixon Presidential Library and Museum. "Dealing with Disaster: 50 Years After Hurricane Agnes." September 8, 2022. www.nixonfoundation.org.

The Richmond Flood: a Unique Picture Magazine Providing a Graphic Account of the Events of June 22, 1972 and Following Days in Richmond, Virginia, and Her Sister Cities. Lubbock, TX: C.F. Boone, 1972.

Silver, Christopher. *Twentieth-Century Richmond: Planning, Politics, and Race*. Knoxville: University of Tennessee Press, 1984.

Virginia Department of Conservation and Recreation, Division of Natural Heritage. *Overview of the Physiography and Vegetation of Virginia*, 2021.

https://www.dcr.virginia.gov/natural-heritage/natural-communities/
document/ncoverviewphys-veg.pdf.

Virginia Museum of History and Culture. "The Regions of Virginia."
https://virginiahistory.org.

Weber, Anna. "50 Years After Hurricane Agnes: What Have We Learned?"
Natural Resources Defense Council, June 21, 2022. https://www.nrdc.org.

Weinkle, Jessica, Chris Landsea, Douglas Collins, Rade Musulin, Ryan
P. Crompton, Philip J. Klotzbach and Roger A. Peilke Jr. "Normalized
Hurricane Damage in the United States: 1900–2017." *Nature Sustainability*
1 (December 2018): 808–13.

INDEX

ABOUT THE AUTHOR

Earnie Porta received his master's degree in history from George Mason University and his doctorate in history from Georgetown University. He has served multiple terms as the mayor of the Town of Occoquan, Virginia, and is on the board of several historical organizations in Prince William County. In 2010 he published a work on Occoquan in Arcadia Publishing's Images of America series.

Visit us at
www.historypress.com